A Best H...

The Frugal Senior

Hundreds of Creative Ways to Stretch a Dollar!

by

Rich Gray

Quill
Driver
Books

Sanger, California

Printed in the United States of America

Published by Quill Driver Books/Word Dancer Press, Inc.
1254 Commerce Boulevard
Sanger, California 93657

559-876-2170 • 1-800-497-4904 • FAX 559-876-2180

QuillDriverBooks.com

Quill Driver Books titles may be purchased in quantity at special discounts for educational, fund-raising, business, or promotional use.
Please contact Special Markets, Quill Driver Books/Word Dancer Press, Inc. at the above address, toll-free at 1-800-497-4909
or by e-mail: Info@QuillDriverBooks.com

Quill Driver Books/Word Dancer Press, Inc. project cadre:
Kathy Chillemi, Dave Marion, Stephen Blake Mettee

To order another copy of this book, please call
1-800-497-4909

Library of Congress Cataloging-in-Publication Data
Gray, Rich.
  The frugal senior / by Rich Gray.
    p. cm.
  ISBN 1-884956-49-1
  1. Older people--Finance, Personal. 2. Saving and investment.
I. Title.
HG179.G725 2005
332.0240084'6--dc22   2005024749

A lot of my interest in this and similar topics I can trace directly back to Helen and Scott Nearing. This book is dedicated to their memory.

Contents

Introduction

Frugal. To many, the very word conjures up an image of Scrooge counting coins in a dimly-lit back room while his assistant shivers upfront for lack of coal. Synonyms such as "tightwad," "cheapskate," and "miserly" spring to mind. In our throwaway society, where debt skyrockets, landfills fill, and the "consumerism clamor" spills relentlessly from every television, radio, and print publication, the term "frugal" has become much-maligned. Unjustly, I would add.

The concept of frugality is not a new one. People throughout the ages have sought to live better within their means, and that's really what it comes down to today: finding creative ways to save money so that you realize more happiness and make real strides towards achieving your long-term goals. Many embrace frugality out of necessity; there is just not enough money coming in to address the needs of their families. Others see the benefits that frugality brings to the environment in terms of cutting down on waste, be it garbage, energy, water, etc. Still others recognize the "consumerism clamor" for what it is: a giant trap with an insatiable appetite for your income, time, and sanity.

It is impossible to keep up with the Joneses. They are currently spending themselves into a hole trying to keep up with you. A better way is to embrace those things which can save you money, reducing stress and leading to happier, more enriching lives. Tightwad? Hardly. Frugal? Proudly!

About This Book

Let's be frank: Frugality is ultimately about altering your life. This book attempts to make this change as painless as possible with hundreds of tips, each one geared towards saving you money in areas such as travel, utilities, the holidays and clothing. The casually frugal will get the most out of this book by opening it at random and daily selecting a tip that they can incorporate into their own lives. Frugal warriors will be more inclined to take one chapter at a time and change the entire way that they look at whole sections of their lives.

Whichever approach you take, you'll find within these pages a new way of living, a new way of *thinking*, that can have profound effects on the quality of your life. Welcome to frugality.

1

Around The House

For the solid majority of us, our houses are our most valuable possessions, and trying to keep a house up and running can be a daunting financial task. This chapter offers up a hodgepodge of tips that can help to ease this burden through the use of cleaning strategies for everything from carpets to chimneys, to tips on repairing and maintaining appliances, furniture, and more.

Make the Most of Your Cleaning Supplies

Let's face it: Manufacturers of cleaning supplies want to sell their products, so the directions they give you for use may be overly generous in terms of what will work best and cheapest. Experiment with the amount of product you use, gradually working down from the recommended amount to the point where the product ceases to work, then nudge the amount up a little bit. This will save you the most amount of money while still ensuring a product that "works as advertised."

Vinegar in the Kitchen

Vinegar has more uses than just for cooking in the kitchen. To boost the grease-cutting power of cheap dish soaps, add half a cup or so of vinegar to dish water. Similarly, you can use it in the dishwasher to help break down buildup; just run a cup of vinegar through the entire cycle every month. Vinegar also makes an excellent cleaner and disinfectant for cutting boards.

Deodorize and Clean Your Microwave

Odors from bacon and other foods can linger in microwaves and effect the taste of everything cooked. You can easily deodorize microwaves by placing a small bowl of baking soda in them between uses. To clean "baked on" food in a microwave, place a bowl with water into the microwave, heat it to the boiling point and then wipe down the inside of the machine with a towel. The boiling water will loosen any food particles, making it easier to wipe them away.

Sparkling Clean Dishes, Cheaply

You needn't spend tons on expensive dishwasher detergents or additives to get sparkling clean, clear, and odor-free dishes. Just add two teaspoons of vinegar to each load you run.

Bottled Hand Soap Strategies

If you use the handy bottles of hand soap, don't throw the old one away when you buy a new one. Split the new with the old and dilute both by half with water. They'll work the same and last twice as long that way.

An Inexpensive Alternative to Glass Cleaner

You can save a lot on window cleaners such as Windex by using a low cost alternative: windshield washer fluid. Wait until the windshield washer fluid goes on sale and then stock up and use it to refill your window cleaner bottles. Each refill will cost you pennies as opposed to the several dollars you would normally pay for a replacement bottle of glass cleaner.

Glass Cleaner Alternative II

Another inexpensive Windex alternative is to make your own. Combine one half teaspoon of liquid soap, three tablespoons vinegar, and two cups of water. Store it in a spray bottle.

Saving in the Shower

You can save a lot on expensive bathroom cleaners later on by wiping down the shower each time you're done using it.

Tub and Sink Cleaner Replacement

Try using baking soda as a replacement tub and sink scouring powder. Not only is it inexpensive, but it won't scratch tub and sink surfaces. It's also a much more friendly cleanser for those with chemical allergies.

Remove Lint from Hair Dryers

When lint starts to clog up the back of your hair dryer, you can easily remove it by dipping a cotton swab in alcohol and applying it to the lint. The lint should come right off.

Remove Build-Up from Humidifiers and Steamers

To help clean humidifiers and steamers and remove mineral deposits that can build up over time, try running them with a combination of one pint of three-percent hydrogen peroxide to one gallon of water.

Keep Light Fixtures Clean

Dirt and dust on light fixtures can absorb a lot of the light emitted by light bulbs. Get the most out of your lighting dollar by keeping all light fixtures clean. You may even be able to drop down to a lower wattage bulb if the level of "pre-clean" light was sufficient for your needs.

Keep Your Chimney Clean

A good way to keep your chimney clean is to occasionally throw a handful of salt (sodium chloride) into the fire. The salt combines with the water released from the wood to create an acid that can help to dissolve light creosote. Do not attempt this with metal chimneys, however, as sodium chloride is corrosive to metal.

Polish for Copper

An easy polish for copper can be found in your refrigerator in the form of catsup. Simply rub catsup all over the copper item, let it stand for five minutes and then rinse it off with hot water.

Polish for Chrome

Chrome can be polished by crumpling up a piece of aluminum foil and rubbing it over the surface you wish to polish. If the chrome is rusted, try dipping the aluminum foil in a carbonated beverage, such as Coke, first.

Removing Mildew

To remove mildew from fabrics and leathers, try using a little chlorine bleach.

Homemade Furniture Polish

Mix any kind of vegetable oil with a little lemon juice to polish furniture. It will give the furniture a lemon-scented shine.

Save On Exterminator/Rug Cleaning Trip Charges

Getting your house exterminated or your carpets professionally cleaned? Get in contact with your neighbors and see if you can team up with someone to get your bugs/carpets done together and possibly save yourself a full trip charge (check with the company first to make sure they'll honor such an arrangement).

Removing Blood Stains from Carpeting

Heaven forbid you ever need to use this tip, but if you ever get blood on carpeting, it can be easily removed by placing an ice cube on the stain for a few minutes. Then scrub downward into the stain with a bit of force, and the stain should come right up.

An Inexpensive Air Freshener

Don't give in to the hype of all the expensive plug-in, spray, or table based air freshening systems. Simply squeeze a few drops of lemon juice into the bag of your vacuum cleaner and each time you run it, voila! A nice clean, lemony scent will waft throughout your house.

Removing Water Marks from Table Tops

If you're suffering from water marks on your otherwise fine polished table tops, try dissolving paraffin shavings in olive or cooking oil, then rub the mixture into the mark. Be sure to rub in one direction only.

Repair Scratches in Furniture

If your polished furniture has been scratched, try the following fix: Take a shelled walnut and rub it into the scratches. After a few seconds, most scratches will disappear!

Removing Heel Marks from Floors

To remove black heel marks from floors, try rubbing the marks with a simple pencil eraser.

Remove Candle Wax from Carpets

An ugly clot of wax hardened into your carpeting may lead you to believe that the best way to fix the problem is just to toss the whole carpet into the nearest Dumpster, but there is an easy fix that you can use to rid any rug of wax. You'll need a clean cloth (or even a paper bag) and a warm iron to use this frugal tip. Simply place the cloth over the wax and gently rub the iron over it. The iron will melt the wax, which will then be absorbed by the cloth. Keep moving the cloth around so that "fresh" areas cover the remaining wax to pick up all of it. If there is still a slight grease stain on the carpet after all the wax has been blotted up, sprinkle a little baking soda onto it, let stand overnight, and then vacuum it up.

Trouble with Chewing Gum

Facing a situation where chewing gum is fused completely into

To remove black heel marks from floors, try rubbing the marks with a simple pencil eraser.

rugs, clothing etc.? One way to remove it is to use turpentine to break down the gum. Other substances you could try include benzene or other hydrofluoric acid. It probably goes without saying, but make sure you rinse after using any of these substances.

Removing Glue and Other Sticky Residue

There are many substances you can use to remove the residue left behind by the likes of stickers and decals, many of them oil-based. The first is vegetable oil itself. Saturate the residue with the oil and then rub it off. Other things you can try include mayonnaise, peanut butter, and nail polish remover.

Unclogging Drains

Before resorting to caustic and expensive drain cleaners, try the following to unclog drains: Pour one quarter cup baking soda down the drain, followed by one half cup vinegar. After the fizzing stops, flush the drain with boiling water. While this method probably won't do much for hardcore clogs, the chemical reaction created by the baking soda and vinegar can help to break up lesser ones.

A Frugal Fix for Dull Scissors

Don't pay several dollars to get scissors sharpened by a professional. To sharpen your own, take a sheet of fine-grade sandpaper and use the scissors to make several cuts into it (six to eight should do).

Sharpening Coffee Grinder Blades

To sharpen the blades of your coffee grinder, place a cup or so of uncooked rice into the grinder and whir it up for a few seconds. This method will also help to clean the grinder.

Loosening Rusted Bolts

To loosen rusted-on bolts, soak a cloth in carbonated water and wrap it around the bolt. Leave it for a few minutes, and the bolt should loosen right up.

Appliances: To Repair or Replace?

When it comes time to decide whether to repair or replace an ailing appliance, there are several things to consider. First, get an estimate and weigh the cost of repair versus the cost of outright replacement. Consider the overall age and mechanical condition of the appliance, and what sorts of other repairs you may face one, two, or five years down the road. Also, take into account the fact that a new appliance may be considerably more energy efficient than your old one. While one always hates to go with something new when something old can be salvaged, things like appliances do eventually break down and have to be replaced. Eking out another year or two via a costly repair may not be the most cost-efficient way to go.

Repair as Much as You Can Yourself ... Eventually

You should try to repair as many of your household appliances yourself as you can. If you lack the necessary skills or expertise, look into taking an introductory household maintenance repair course at your local community college, high school, or technical institute. The class will pay for itself the first time you actually fix something yourself, as opposed to calling a professional. When you should *not* try to tackle repairs yourself is when something is still under warranty. In most cases, an appliance still under warranty will be covered for both parts and service in case something goes wrong. If you try to make the repairs yourself, you may void the warrantee. Check the fine print on the warranty carefully before attempting any repairs yourself on something that might still be covered.

Appliance Manuals: Your Guides to Savings

Select a spot in your home to store all the manuals that come with appliance and other household items, and take the time to occasionally glance through them to familiarize yourself with any maintenance or use recommendations contained within them. Following a manufacturer's recommendations will help you to keep your appliances in prime condition and keep them running longer. Also, before breaking down and calling a professional for, an appliance that is acting up, consult the "problems" or "troubleshooting" section of the manual for possible easy fixes, such as replacing blown internal fuses, finding the location of the reset button, etc.

Getting Recommendations on Repairmen

If you've reached the point where an appliance repair is beyond your abilities, don't settle for the first person you find in the phone book to do the job. Get recommendations from family members, friends, and neighbors. When you have obtained a couple of names this way, call them up, have them take a look at the appliance and give you an estimate in writing on what each will charge you to fix the problem. With this information in hand, you should be able to select someone whom you trust and who can save you money on the repairs.

Borrowing Little Used Items

If you have something you use only occasionally around your house (ex. a rug cleaner), consider borrowing it from friends instead of buying it. Just make sure that you return the favor (consider it frugal karma).

Have Screwdriver, Will Assemble

Buy furniture like bookcases, end tables, and the like in an unassembled form. Such things come complete with everything you need to put them together (including directions) and it is generally cheaper and easier to transport unassembled furniture than the pre-assembled variety.

Heating Your House Via the Shower

During cold weather, don't let the heat from your shower water go down the drain. Put the plug in the tub while taking your shower, and let the water cool completely before draining it. It may seem insignificant, but it really can help to add heat to your house (not to mention, a fair amount of humidity).

Absorbing Bathroom Odors

Avoid the need to use spray deodorizers in the bathroom by keeping a small bowl of baking soda behind the toilet.

A Substitute for Mothballs

In place of mothballs, try taking a few leftover slivers of soap and placing them in a vented plastic bag. Place the bag in with your seasonal clothing when you store it. This will not only keep moths at bay, but also give the clothes a great smell.

Try a Non-Toxic Ant Repellant

If you know where ants are coming into your house, you can easily and cheaply keep them at bay by sprinkling cinnamon or black pepper in front of the access point. Ants won't cross "hot" spices such as these.

Cockroach Solution

You can handle annoying cockroach problems by mixing up a solution of equal parts of boric acid (found in hardware stores) and sugar, then sprinkling the mixture into crevices, under sinks, or around any other places that cockroaches gather. While this solution is less toxic than most commercial cockroach chemicals, boric acid can still be harmful if ingested in a large enough quantity, so care should be taken if you use it around pets or grandchildren.

Keep Kitty Litter Fresh

To keep kitty litter smelling fresh, try adding either a little baking soda or baby powder to it on a regular basis.

Kitty Litter—More Uses

Kitty litter isn't just for, well, the obvious. It works very well as a cheap alternative to sand or salt on icy walks, and works as well to soak up oil and other car fluids that spill in your garage or driveway.

Recycle Tissue Boxes

You can get more use out of tissue boxes by putting them to another task after they are empty: as storage for plastic grocery bags. Place the bags in the box as you get them, and when you need one just pull it out like you would the original contents of the box.

Uses for Newspapers

Before recycling your newspapers, you can put them to a variety of uses. Newspapers can be used as garden mulch, to wash windows, as a shipping replacement for packing peanuts, as a cheap wrapping paper for presents, as fire starters, trash can liners . . . the list is nearly endless.

Frequent Home Maintenance Websites

If you have Internet access, you have a wealth of frugal resources at your fingertips (see the Other Resources chapter for more on this). This includes a number of home maintenance sites that offer tips, tutorials, and advice on keeping up all aspects of your home. The best way to find something specific (i.e., how to fix a leaky faucet) is to enter your question or the name of an item into a search engine such as Google (www.google.com) and sift through the results until you find what you're looking for. The following sites are particularly valuable for the do-it-yourselfer:

DoItYourself.com
http://www.doityourself.com

Home Maintenance and Repair
http://web1.msue.msu.edu/msue/imp/mod02/master02.html

Repair-Home.com
http://www.repair-home.com

2
Automotive & Transportation

Next to a house, automobiles are the most expensive possession in most peoples' lives. This isn't too surprising, particularly when you consider everything that goes into owning a car or truck. First, you have to purchase one, new or used. Then you have to insure it and maintain it, all the while shelling out a steady stream of cash on gas to keep it running. It can all add up fast, but the following tips can save you considerably when it comes to automotive bills. Among the topics covered here: buying strategies for new and used vehicles; driving strategies you can employ to save gas; how to maintain your vehicle properly; suggestions for saving on insurance premiums; and a variety of other ideas to save you money, from making your own car wax to planning for extended car trips.

When to Shop for Cars

Consider shopping for a new or used car near the end of the month. Car salesmen, used or otherwise, try to meet certain quotas each month, and if they are struggling to meet that month's particular quota, they may be willing to make better deals.

To Buy or Lease?

Based on the lower payments, you may be tempted to lease rather than purchase a vehicle, but make sure you read the contract very carefully. Lease contracts vary widely in terms of trade-in allowances, down payments you'll need to come up with up-front, end of lease payments, and the possibility of a variety of fees that you can be assessed for driving too many miles, excess wear and tear on the vehicle, etc. Add to this the fact that, at the end of the lease, you won't even own the vehicle! If you can swing the slightly higher payments, you'll be able to build equity and preserve peace of mind by avoiding leases.

Price Shop for New Cars

If you already know what model (and what features) you want in a new car, don't hesitate to contact several local dealers for price quotes. Be sure to let them know you are price shopping; it's amazing how many rebates and incentives *that* information can shake loose from a salesman. You can also comparison shop, research vehicles, and get price quotes on web sites such as:

CarsDirect (http://www.carsdirect.com) and
AutoTrader.com (http://www.autotrader.com).

Purchase Used Vehicles from Someone You Know

If at all possible, try to purchase used vehicles only from someone you know or trust. You'll be more likely to pay a lower price, and the seller will be much more willing to point out any known problems with the vehicle.

Blue Book Used Vehicles

Long used by insurance companies, banks, and other lending

institutions, the *Kelly Blue Book* is the standard when it comes to used vehicle pricing. Before purchasing a used car or truck, always check the *Blue Book* to make sure that the asking price is a fair one. Obviously, if you're looking to sell a used car or truck, this is also a very valuable tool when it comes to deciding what price to ask for. You can find a copy of the *Kelly Blue Book* at your library, bank, or credit union, or you can access it online at http://www.kbb.com.

Used Cars – Get a Second Opinion

Regardless of where you're looking to buy a used car, don't just take the seller's word on the vehicle's health. All vehicles should be run past a mechanic whom you trust, not only to identify existing problems, but also to pinpoint any repairs that you'll likely be facing a few months down the road.

Avoid Idling

Needless to say, a car that is running but not moving is just wasting gas. Try to avoid letting your vehicle idle. A couple of areas you can target with this tip include "warming up" your car (something that isn't really necessary with vehicles these days, unless it is extremely cold) and sitting in traffic (if you're stuck and not moving for more than a couple of minutes, shut off the engine).

Gas-Saving Strategies

There are a number of things you can do to save on the amount of gas you use. Try taking the bus to work, car pool, or if possible, ride a bike; the exercise alone will be a huge benefit. If your vehicle really sucks down the gas, consider getting one that is more fuel efficient. You can also get better gas mileage by driving slower (55 or under) and accelerating gradually.

Reasons Not To Speed

Speeding while driving is a big no-no. Not only is it dangerous, but if you're caught, you face the cost of both a speeding ticket and increased insurance rates.

If Possible, Avoid Gridlock while Heading to Work

If you have some flexibility about when you are required to report for work each day, consider changing the time to avoid the morning and evening rush hours. Driving during these times will usually result in longer commute times, and being stuck in slow or stalled traffic will greatly affect your gas mileage.

Gas Price Comparison

It may seem obvious, but definitely keep an eye on gas prices at competing stations in your area. You might think that they will all roughly be the same, but sometimes you can find a station that offers considerable savings over others. Plus, even a penny or two difference in the price of a gallon of gas can add up to quite a bit over the course of a year.

Is High-Grade Gas Necessary?

Unless your car manual specifically calls for it, don't fall into the trap of buying higher grade gas because you think it will benefit your vehicle. Most vehicles these days are designed to work very well with regular unleaded, and higher grades will result in few benefits, while robbing you of several dollars each and every time you go to fill your tank.

An Overweight Car is a Gas Hog

Is your trunk filled with extraneous stuff that you feel you may someday need? Consider storing this in your garage. Every pound you place in your vehicle is another pound that the engine needs to work to haul around, which equals a decrease in fuel efficiency.

To Reduce Drag, Keep Windows Closed

Consider keeping your vehicle's windows closed when you are traveling at high speed, as open windows can result in considerable drag and reduce your gas mileage. If you desire a breeze, try opening the vehicle's passive air vents.

Remove Ski and Other Racks from Vehicle Roofs

Do you have a removable ski rack on the top of your vehicle? If you're not planning to use it in the near future, consider removing it. Ski racks (and all form of roof racks, actually) can result in considerable drag on your vehicle, which can adversely affect your gas mileage.

AC Strategies

Air conditioning in a vehicle is a wonderful thing when the temperatures soar, but be aware that using the air conditioner can greatly reduce your gas mileage. The best way to use a car air conditioner is to set it at the lowest setting that makes you comfortable, and turn it off when you've reached that comfort level. The vehicle's fan will continue to circulate the cool air for some time, and you can continue to add "spurts" of coolness as the air within the car starts to heat up.

Regulate Tire Pressure to Save Money on Gas

Your tire pressure is very important in terms of safety, but did you know that it also can help you save money on gas? Overinflated tires can reduce the fuel efficiency of your car, so check them often to make sure they are within the manufacturer's specifications.

Double (Triple, etc.) Up On Car Runs

Keep a running list of things you have to do when you take your car out so that you are not running to town every day to do just one thing. Combining as many chores as possible into a trip will not only save you money, but also precious time.

Beware of Road Salt in Northern Areas

If you live in a northern area where they often use salt to keep the roads manageable, try to spray down the underside of your vehicle whenever the temperature rises above freezing. Salt is one of metal's worst enemies, and removing it will help to keep your vehicle rust free and increase its lifetime.

Find a Mechanic Before You Need One

The time to begin searching for a good mechanic is before you need one, and one of the best ways to find a good one (and avoid a bad one) is to ask your friends and neighbors for recommendations. Evaluate the mechanic you select by taking your car in for light service work. Once you've found a mechanic you both trust and like, continue to take your car to him/her whenever necessary to become a "regular" customer. When your vehicle reaches the point where it needs some serious work (and they all do eventually), you'll be glad you put the time into finding a mechanic you're comfortable with.

The time to begin searching for a good mechanic is before you need one.

Pre-Inspect Your Vehicle

Before taking your vehicle in for inspection, check it out and do any simple repairs yourself. Such things as burnt-out taillights and damaged wipers will need to be replaced before you can get a new inspection sticker, and you will save quite a bit by making these repairs yourself.

Keep Your Car Tuned Up

From the "break a few eggs to make an omelet" department comes this tip: Keep your car tuned up. A car in optimum running condition will easily save enough in gas and potential future problems to pay off the cost of the tune-up, and much more in the long run.

Keep an Auto Log

Consider keeping an auto log for your vehicle. This is a simple notebook in which you record anything regarding repairs, maintenance, or operation of your vehicle, from major parts replacement to fill-ups and fluid additions. Not only will this put all your vehicle's service information at your fingertips in case you need to visit a mechanic, but keeping a close eye on the log will also alert you to potential problems (i.e., if your gas mileage is decreasing or oil/fluid consumption is increasing, it may be a sign of some pending issue that you can save money on by dealing with early).

Search Out Coupons for Simple Car Services

While its always better (from a money perspective) to do simple car maintenance, such as oil changes and tire rotations yourself, sometimes this just isn't possible. You can often find coupons for such things in your local newspaper or phone book that can save you a few dollars.

Car Repairs? Consider the Local Trade School

Do what you can in terms of repairs on your own car, but if you run up against something too difficult to tackle, consider taking it to a local trade school or the vocational tech section of a local high school. They will generally only charge for parts.

Change Oil Frequently in Older Cars

While it's important to regularly change the oil in all vehicles, this is particularly important for older cars. Oil consumption increases as a vehicle ages, so make sure that you change the oil every three months or 3000 miles, whichever comes first.

Protect Battery Terminals from Corrosion

You can cut down on battery post corrosion in your car by coating the posts with Vaseline. Just be sure that the car engine has been off for a while and is cool before doing this.

Burning Off Excess Engine Carbon Deposits

If you find that carbon is building up in your car's carburetor, here's an inexpensive but effective way to combat it. Disconnect the vacuum tube from the intake manifold and substitute it with another tube leading to a container of hydrogen peroxide. Let this be drawn into the idling motor, and the excess oxygen will burn off any built-up carbon deposits in the engine.

Shop Around for Car Insurance

Prices for auto insurance can fluctuate greatly from company to company, so be sure to get price quotes from several different companies before deciding on one to go with. Websites, such as

Progressive.com (http://www.progressive.com/), offer an easy way to compare quotes from several different companies.

Buy All Your Insurance from One Provider

Already have some form of insurance through a specific company? Contact them to see if they offer a discount if you also use them to insure your car. Definitely take the numbers they give you and shop around, however, to make sure that their "discounted" rate is the lowest one available to you.

Raise Your Insurance Deductible

Contact your insurance agent about raising your auto insurance deductible. While you would end up paying more out-of-pocket in the event of an accident, you could end up saving a sizable amount on your monthly payments.

Drop Collision on Older Cars

If your vehicle is paid off, consider dropping collision insurance from your policy. To figure out if this is a worthwhile thing to do, take into account your car's current value (see the tip concerning the *Kelly Blue Book* earlier in this chapter for more information on how to do this) and contrast that with what you're paying for collision insurance, plus your deductible.

Prices for auto insurance can fluctuate greatly from company to company, so be sure to get price quotes from several different companies before deciding on one to go with.

Other Insurance Discounts

When shopping for auto insurance, make sure you grill your agent regarding any possible discount for which you might be eligible. Many companies offer discounts for a wide range of things, including:

- Seniors
- Clean driving record
- Antitheft devices
- Low annual mileage
- Air bags
- Anti-lock brakes
- Daytime running lights
- Long term customers

Avoid Expensive Carwashes

Wash your own car. Better, get the grandchildren to wash your car. Best, pick a really hot day and *join* your grandchildren in washing the car. Just remember to point the hose in the direction of the car on occasion.

Keep Windshields Ice and Frost-Free

Keep your car windows ice and frost-free in the winter by combining three parts vinegar to one part water and then coating the windows with this solution. This is a great aid to those living in winter climates who have neither a garage nor a carport.

Low Cost Antifreeze

Looking for a low cost antifreeze that will be safe at temperatures of up (down) to 60 degrees below zero? Try old motor oil thinned with kerosene.

Homemade Car Wax

You can easily save a few dollars by making your own car wax (this also makes a nice gift for the car buff in your life). All you need is one cup of carnauba or coconut oil, one cup beeswax, and one quarter cup olive oil. Combine all ingredients and melt over a low flame, stirring occasionally to combine the wax and oils. When melted, pour the mixture into a tin or other container and let cool, and then use it as you would any car wax.

Plan for a Road Trip

Kill the convenience store cravings! Plan the night ahead for any sort of an extended road trip by packing munchies and beverages. One good trick for the latter is to freeze water bottles (leave enough space in the bottle for the ice to expand). The ice will melt throughout the day and not only keep your food cool but also provide you with a steady supply of cold water, and you'll save money by staying out of overpriced convenience stores.

Take a Class

You can really save money doing a lot of your own car maintenance, but if you've never done it before, it can be a bit daunting. Check local trade schools, vocational tech centers, community colleges, or your AAA chapter to find out if there are any inexpensive classes on simple car maintenance near you. A lot of the skills necessary to maintain your vehicle are very easy to learn and will quickly pay for the cost of the class.

3
Health & Beauty

You can easily spend vast amounts of money stocking your medicine and beauty cabinets with the latest and (the companies assure us) greatest health and beauty products. Or, you could take the frugal path and "shop" for such items a little closer to home: in your kitchen. Many items, such as vinegar, olive oil, and honey, have built-in properties that make them ideal choices for a wide range of health and beauty needs.

This chapter looks at a number of health and beauty uses for some of these commonly-found items, as well as offering a number of other frugal tips in the areas of health and beauty.

Don't Leave the Doctor's Office Empty-Handed

Pharmaceutical companies are constantly plying doctors with free drug samples. Next time you visit your doctor, ask if he or she has any samples that would be applicable to your current health situation.

Shop Around for Medicine

The price of medications can vary wildly from pharmacy to pharmacy, so definitely call around to price specific medications. Another option is to contact mail-order pharmacies to see what they are charging (keeping in mind that you'll also be paying shipping/handling on top of the medications' costs).

Save Money on Vitamins

Don't feel you have to spring for the latest designer vitamin or mineral supplement. Many generic vitamins are pretty much the same as the name-brand version that sells for three to four times as much. Compare ingredient labels.

Cheap & Effective Burn Treatment

When it comes to treating light burns, you really can't do much better than the simple aloe plant. Packed into each aloe plant are over seventy-five different vitamins, minerals, amino acids, enzymes, and other compounds that help to kill pain and heal burned skin. Keep one or two plants in the kitchen for when you need them. To use aloe plants, just break off a leaf and apply the inside gel directly to the burn.

Bee Sting First Aid

To take the pain out of a bee sting, there are several homemade treatments you can try. Wet tobacco works well, as does cutting an onion and applying it directly to the sting. Something else you can try is to make a paste of baking soda and vinegar and apply it directly to the sting area.

Sunburn First Aid

Suffering from the effects of a little too much sun? To take the itch and pain away, there are several things you can try, including soaking in a bathtub with oatmeal or applying white vinegar, aloe (either in packaged gel form or from the plant itself), or baking soda to the burn area.

Make Your Own Ice Pack

You can make your own ice pack by combining one part rubbing alcohol and two parts water, then filling a plastic bag or two with this mixture and freezing it. The alcohol keeps the pack from freezing completely, so you can easily mold it to any part of your body.

Uses for Witch Hazel

Introduced to the first colonists by Native Americans in the Northeast, witch hazel was a staple in most peoples' medicine cabinets throughout the nineteenth century. Witch hazel is derived from the witch hazel shrub that grows in the northeastern United States and parts of Asia, and you can put this frugal substance to any number of health and beauty uses. Because of its healing and soothing properties, it makes a great aftershave, insect bite treatment, or salve to use on sun or wind burns. It can be used as a deodorant, or it can be applied to the face to help clean, soothe, and tone the skin. You can even apply it to poison oak, poison sumac, or poison ivy outbreaks to help dry up blistered skin.

You can make your own ice pack by combining one part rubbing alcohol and two parts water, then filling a plastic bag or two with this mixture and freezing it.

Vinegar as a Tonic

You can decrease your appetite and improve your overall feeling of well-being by drinking a tonic of one teaspoon of cider vinegar to one glass of water. Add a little honey for taste, if you're so inclined.

Vinegar and Lemon in Hair Care

If you color your own hair, using white vinegar, diluted with cold water for the final rinse, will help to seal in the colors. Hair can also be streaked or highlighted by drawing a cut lemon across sections of it and then going out into the sun for a short time to let the lemon juice "bleach" into the hair.

Hot Oil Treatment from the 'Fridge

You can deep treat dry or damaged hair using an item found in most refrigerators: mayonnaise. To do this, massage the mayonnaise into your hair and scalp, then wrap your head in a warm towel and let it sit for fifteen minutes. After fifteen minutes, rinse out the mayonnaise using warm water.

Deep Condition Your Hair

You can easily deep condition your hair by applying aloe vera gel and letting it sit for up to half an hour, then rinsing and shampooing.

Deep Condition Your Hair, II

Another item that can help your hair is raw eggs. Beat them thoroughly, apply the beaten eggs to your hair and let set for five to ten minutes before rinsing.

Hairspray Alternatives

You can save money, and perhaps cut down on some of the chemicals you expose yourself to, by trying a couple of different hairspray alternatives. For the first, simply add a small amount of sugar to boiling water. Stir the mixture until the sugar is completely dissolved, let it cool, and place it into a spray bottle. Another option is to add a cut-up orange or lemon to boiling water, reduce the heat to a simmer, and let it cook for five to ten minutes. Strain the liquid, let it cool, and add it to a spray bottle.

Clarifying Hair Treatment

To "clarify" your hair, try mixing one quarter cup baking soda with one quarter cup molasses. Store this mixture in a bottle, then once a week work a little of it into your hair, letting it sit for up to half an hour before rinsing and shampooing.

Student Hair Cuts

You may be taking a bit to chance using this approach, but for a cheap haircut, look to your nearest beauty or hair-dressing school. Technically, your head will be a learning tool, but the students are carefully supervised, the haircuts are inexpensive, and you can usually find Saturday appointments easily. You can also use this tactic to find inexpensive services offered by schools in other areas, such as dentistry and massage.

Olive Oil as a Skin Conditioner

Olive oil can be used in any number of ways to soften or condition skin. For the hands, moisten them and then rub a small amount of oil into them until the oil is absorbed. Feet can also be made softer by rubbing oil into them, then wearing socks and letting the heat/oil do their magic. You can also make a night cream by combining one half cup olive oil, one quarter cup vinegar, and one quarter cup water.

The Olive Oil and Sugar Facial

For a great, natural facial, try wetting your face and then massaging olive oil into the skin. Follow this up by scrubbing about a teaspoon of sugar into the face. Wipe off any excess with a warm, wet towel to complete the facial.

Yogurt as an Exfoliant

Yogurt . . . good in you, good on you. The lactic acid bacteria in yogurt makes it very effective at dissolving dead skin cells. To use, rinse your face with warm water, and then massage in a tablespoon of plain yogurt. Let this sit for a few minutes before rinsing the yogurt off with warm water.

Honey as an Antibacterial

Honey is a natural antibacterial, and you can use this fact to help combat any problem areas on your face. To use, moisten the skin with warm water and then massage a tablespoon of honey into it. Let this sit for a few minutes, then rinse off with warm water.

Egg Whites as a Skin Firmer

For a natural, frugal skin firmer, whisk up a few egg whites and spread them on your face. Let the mixture dry, and then rinse off with warm water.

Retire Age Spots

Rub lemon juice into age spots and freckles to help them fade.

Another way to fade age spots is by rubbing equal parts of onion juice and vinegar into them. Be patient, though. Both of these methods can take a couple of weeks before you start to see results.

Bathe Like Cleopatra

Legend has it that Cleopatra maintained her beautiful skin by taking milk baths, and science now has proven why you should too. Like yogurt, milk contains lactic acid, which can help to dissolve the glue holding dead skin together, resulting in a cleanser that can reach deeply into the layers of your skin. To make a milk bath, add two to four cups of milk or buttermilk to your bathwater. Soak in the bath for twenty minutes, then gently rub your skin with a washcloth or loofah to remove the dead skin. Warning: Those allergic to milk or who are lactose intolerant should not try this beauty treatment.

Vinegar, After the Bath

Mix equal parts of vinegar and water for use as an afterbath neutralizer to remove soap alkalis from the skin.

Make Your Own Unscented Bath Salts

Epsom bath salts come packed with a heck of a lot of health and beauty potential. They can lower blood pressure, elevate your mood by raising the body's serotonin level, exfoliate skin, and help to smooth its rough patches. They can also be a bit pricey . . . unless you make your own. What follows are two recipes for making your own bath salts, the first one unscented:

- 2 cups Epsom salts
- 5 tablespoons cocoa butter

Place the cocoa butter in a blender or coffee grinder and blend into a fine powder. Combine the powder with the Epsom salts and store in a dry container, such as a glass jar. To use, add one to two cups to running bath water.

Make Your Own Floral Bath Salts

The following bath-salt recipe packs a bit more of a punch due to the inclusion of aromatherapy or essential oil:

- •2 cups Epsom salts
- •2 tablespoons pickling salt
- •35 drops floral essential oil, such as ylang ylang
- •5 tablespoons powdered milk

Combine the Epsom salts and powdered milk in a bowl. In another bowl, combine the oil and pickling salt, and mix thoroughly. Add the oil mixture to the Epsom salts/milk mixture and blend well. Store in an airtight, dry container. To use, add one to two cups to running bath water.

Extend Your Bubble Bath

There's nothing quite so luxurious as a bubble bath, but it seems to be over all too quickly. To make your bubble bath bubbles last longer (and richer so you use less overall), sprinkle a teaspoon of baking soda into the water.

Olive Oil as a Lip Balm

You can make your own lip balm by melting a little beeswax, combining it with olive oil and pouring the mixture into a tin container to let it set up.

Puffy Eye Cure

If you wake up in the morning with puffy eyes, try this quick and easy remedy: Place slices of potato or cucumber over your closed eyes. Apply a little pressure and let them sit for several minutes.

Get More Life from Razor Blades

Razor blades will stay sharp much longer if you store them blade-down in a cup with a little vegetable oil in the bottom between uses. Just be sure to rinse the oil from the blades before use.

Pickled Dentures?

Soak dentures in vinegar to help remove plaque, and then brush them with baking soda. The chemical reaction between these two materials will leave dentures shiny and smooth.

A Use for Old Panty Hose

Here's a use for old panty hose: Cut them into one inch rings, and then use them with finger nail polish remover to remove polish from your fingers or toes.

Avoid Department Store Makeup

When you buy makeup from a department store, you're essentially paying top dollar simply for the brand name. You can usually find much cheaper items with the same ingredients at drug stores.

4
Clothing

Whether you're buying, cleaning, or repairing clothing and shoes, this is another area that can take a sizable chunk out of the household budget if you let it. The following tips can help you save money when acquiring clothing, and also help you to get the most life from what you currently own and wear.

Frugal Does Not Mean Cheap

Being frugal when shopping for clothes is not the same as buying cheap clothing. You may save initially on cheap clothing, but if the same clothing is going to rip, fade, or otherwise become unwearable after only a few months, you've really not saved yourself anything. Cheap clothing will provide you with a steady source of rags, though.

Avoid Trendy Clothing

The problem with trendy clothing is that it has a short shelf life (although it frequently comes back into popularity if you wait long enough). To get the most use out of clothing over an extended period of time, try to avoid trendy clothing.

Categorize Your Clothing According to Use

You'll wear out less clothes if you categorize every piece of clothing you own according to its use: work clothes, play clothes, gardening clothes, nice clothes for dining out and special affairs, etc.

Let Your Dryer Do Double Duty

Instead of venting your electric dryer outside and wasting all that heat, try venting it inside. You can buy special capture devices to plug into the end of the hose to catch all the lint, or attach nylon hose to the end of it. ***Note: you can't do this with a gas dryer due to the risk of carbon monoxide poisoning.***

Drying Multiple Loads of Clothes

When drying clothes, try to do two or more loads immediately after each other. After the first load, the dryer will still be warm and the second, third, etc. loads will take less time to dry, using less energy.

Avoid "Stiff Clothes" Line Drying Syndrome

You like the idea of drying clothes on the line (and it certainly is cheaper), but you hate that stiff feel to them? Try drying the clothes for ten minutes or so in the dryer before hanging them on the line. This should leave the clothes much softer, and your pocketbook much heavier.

Try drying the clothes for ten minutes or so in the dryer before hanging them on the line. This should leave the clothes much softer, and your pocketbook much heavier.

Stretching Out Your Dryer Sheets

Make dryer sheets do time and a half by using one each for an individual load, then throwing both into the third load together. The two used ones will work just as well as a single new one.

Dryer Sheet Alternative

Save on dryer sheets by trying the following: Buy a gallon of cheap fabric softener at the store, pour some into a butter or whipped cream tub, and throw a few sponges in with it. When you run a load in the dryer, wring out one of the sponges and throw it in with the load. This will give you an instant, and much less expensive, dryer sheet.

Abandon Ye Dryer

You can save a considerable amount of money every month by foregoing the dryer and air-drying your clothes. In good weather hang everything on the line. In bad weather, try to rig up some sort of a rack system in your laundry room. In the winter, this latter will also help to add humidity to your house. Even if you just air-dry large items, such as jeans and towels, you will save yourself several dryer loads and the cost associated with running them.

Use the "Half" Method

Those recommended portion amounts on such things as clothes detergent, fabric softener, dish soap, shampoo, and other cleaning materials are set by the manufacturer who, surprise surprise, is trying to sell you more of its product. Try halving all recommended amounts and see if this does the job just as well. Most times, you'll find that it will, and you'll save a lot of money.

A Couple of Ironing Tips

You can save electricity when ironing by turning the iron to a lower temperature and placing a sheet of aluminum foil, shiny side up, between the ironing board pad and cover.

Avoid the Iron

You can cut down on a lot of ironing chores by folding clothing straight from the dryer, saving on electricity and time. And, let's face it, the less ironing you have to do, the better.

Fixing Glossy Clothing

Sick of dealing with shiny, glossy clothing? You can fix this by ironing them on the wrong side and using a cloth containing witchhazel extract (instead of water) as a pressing cloth.

Care of Men's Suits

Between dry cleanings, you can press men's suits yourself by using a damp cloth between the fabric and the iron. While they should definitely be dry-cleaned occasionally to help preserve the fibers, once or twice a year should be sufficient.

Women Should Frequent the Men's Department

Women can save a lot of money on the basics by purchasing them in the men's department. Women's clothing often carry a higher price tag than similar men's.

How To Buy Growing Children's Clothing

Buy clothing a little larger than you normally would for grand-children. Pants can be hemmed and then let out when the child is larger (to get rid of the hemline, try a little vinegar and an iron). Shirt sleeves can also be rolled up if they are initially too large. This is one way to get the most out of clothing for a growing child.

Children's Clothing Replacement Policy

Check with stores such as Sears and Kmart to see if they have replacement policies for clothing that you buy for grandchildren. These types of policies state that the store will replace an item of clothing if the child wears it out before outgrowing it. While you may not have a huge use for such a policy, it's nice to know that the option is there for the parents, particularly for abused items, such as jeans.

Matching Cloth To Make Small Repairs

Need to make a small repair to a skirt or pants? Check the inside pocket or hem to see if it matches the repair you need to make. You can use this to make the repair, then replace the inside pocket or hem with any kind of fabric. As it doesn't show, no one will be the wiser.

Button Replacement 101

Missing a button or two? Trying to find a replacement that matches the rest can be not only a needle-in-a-haystack endeavor, but also can be expensive once you do find one. Buy buttons in bulk and merely replace all of the buttons so that they match.

Repairing Clothes Snaps

Having problems with snaps on clothing that won't stay snapped? You might be able to "repair" the problem by taking a hammer and tapping the ball part slightly, so that it will fit more snugly into the socket part. Just start slowly and gently and work up to the point that gets the job done.

Coat Makeovers (aka, Reline, Reline)

If the lining of your coat is getting pretty raggedy, don't immediately toss it out. A coat in otherwise good shape can be relined by a tailor for a fraction of the cost of a new one.

Dealing with Ink Stains

Have an ink stain on a favorite shirt or blouse? Spray the spot with hairspray and rub it in, repeating as necessary until the stain has either disappeared or is blurry. Wash the shirt or blouse as normal, and the stain should be gone.

Washing Clothes To Keep Them Looking Good & Lasting Long

To keep clothes looking their best, wash and rinse dark-colored clothes in cold water, and use a warm wash and cold rinse for light-colored clothes. This will also save you money on your hot water heater. Note that detergents can vary as to their needs and amounts, so be sure to read directions carefully.

Care of Ties

Ties can be sprayed with fabric protector spray so that you'll rarely have to dry-clean them.

To keep clothes looking their best, wash and rinse dark colored-clothes in cold water, and use a warm wash and cold rinse for light-colored clothes.

Polish Your Shoes Before Wearing Them

Polish your shoes before wearing them. This will help to keep them from getting scratches.

Weatherproof Shoes and Pocketbooks

That spray, on leather weather protector isn't just for camping attire any more. Spray shoes and leather pocketbooks to help them ward off the weather and stay in good shape.

Quickly Dry Out Shoes

Wet shoes can be "cured" or dried out by stuffing them full of crumpled newspaper, changing the paper a few times to absorb all the moisture. To be a bit more indelicate, this also works for hot, perspiration-enhanced shoes.

Save Your Heels

You can save your shoe heel from wearing out by having tips put on the bottom of your shoes.

Resole, Resole, Resole!

Don't toss out shoes simply because the soles are shot. Often, you can get them resoled inexpensively, and they'll be like new. Remember that most of the damage that a shoe runs into will be sole-related.

Toss Away the Lint Brush

To eliminate lint on fabrics in the dryer, try the following: Toss an old, clean nylon stocking in with the load, making sure to tie it in a knot so that it won't tangle up and make too much of a mess with socks, etc.

Avoid Dry-Clean Only Clothing

The clothing that comes with a tag declaring it is "Dry-Clean Only"? Call your dry cleaner to price how much it costs to clean an item of that type, and you'll hastily put it back next time you run into such clothing in a store. Dry cleaning is very pricey, and avoiding items that require this particular cleaning method will save you considerably over time.

Air Out Clothing Instead of Cleaning?

So long as you weren't mud wrestling or trying to cap the latest oil gusher on your front lawn, the clothes you are wearing today may not even need to be washed. Clothes that are in good shape can often be "rejuvenated" simply by airing them out (this is particularly true with those items where dry cleaning is recommended). This will not only save on detergent and electricity, but also on wear and tear to the clothing itself.

Adios Mismatched/Orphaned Socks

Say good-bye to mismatched (and orphaned) socks forever by buying the same brand and color of socks. Sure, it's not as much fun, but after every dryer run you'll either have all socks that match up with each other or wind up with a spare on hand for the day another one gets lost.

Clothes that are in good shape can often be "rejuvenated" simply by airing them out (this is particularly true with those items where dry cleaning is recommended).

Uses for Old Coats and Jackets

Never just throw out an old coat or jacket . . . turn it into something new. The fabric from these items make great potholders (make sure you hem them), insoles for boots/shoes, heavy-duty rags, etc.

Apron: Your Life Preserver in the Kitchen

Get into a habit of using an apron every time you cook in the kitchen. Even the most careful of cooks occasionally gets splashed, and an apron will protect your clothes from stains. Actually, aprons *love* stains, so you'll be doing them a favor, as well.

Keep Good Clothes from Getting Wrinkled

Take off good clothes as soon as you get home and hang them up. This will keep them from getting wrinkled and save you the cost of using an iron to press them the next time you use them.

The Best Way To Sell Used Clothing

Don't automatically earmark clothing you're finished with for a yard sale. You'll actually get a better rate of return at a consignment store.

Uses for Hemmed Material

When hemming or cutting a garment, don't toss out the scraps. Use them to make matching hair ties, scarves, cloth belts, etc.

Save with White Towels

Cut down on your need for color-protecting detergents by buying all white towels. This way you can just use regular bleach to wash them.

A Step for Dealing with a New Rag

Before relegating a rag to the rag bin, take a moment to put a hem on it. The rag will last longer, and you won't be filling up lint filters or your plumbing needlessly with rag ravelings. Plus, the rag will just be easier to deal with (no twisted ravelings to untangle… which doesn't seem like it'd be a huge problem, until you add twenty more similar rags to the mix).

5

Computers & the Internet

Computers and the Internet have become indispensable to many of our lives, and this can be another area where you can find yourself spending a lot more than you had planned to. The tips covered in this chapter suggest everything from saving on general computer purchases and usage to online websites where you can find free coupons, reference materials, and even entertainment. It seems fitting to start this off by asking if you even really need a computer.

Do You Really Need a Computer?

If you find yourself using your computer simply to send e-mail and occasionally surf the Internet, consider getting rid of it and using the computers in your local library. This will save you not only on the cost of the computer (when you eventually have to replace it), but also the electricity to run it, Internet Service Provider (ISP) charges, etc. Free e-mail systems from the likes of Yahoo! (http://mail.yahoo.com/), Hotmail (http://www.hotmail.com/), and Google (http://gmail.google.com/) allow you to keep in touch with friends and family via e-mail without needing to have your own computer and ISP. You'll also be able to use these systems to access e-mail from virtually anywhere in the world.

Don't Buy More Computer than You Need

Computers can run the gamut from no-frills, inexpensive models to technological powerhouses stocked with powerful graphics cards, massive memory modules, and top-end computer chips. When you consider the number and range of peripherals you can add to a basic computer system (printers, scanners, web cams, etc.), you begin to see how a computer's costs can quickly balloon. Before you buy a system, sit down and consider realistically what you'll be using it for. In most cases, an inexpensive system that comes bundled with a monitor and printer will meet all your computing needs, and you can always add onto it later if the need arises.

Computer Self-Setup

Avoid offers from companies that sell you a computer and then come out and set it up for you for an additional fee. Computers have reached the point where they come pre-loaded and color coded with instructions, so you should be able to handle the yourself. If it still looks like something from an alien planet, ask friends or relatives for help. Those who know computers can probably get your system up and running in minutes.

Should You Upgrade Your Software?

If you are thinking of upgrading your software to take advantage of the latest and greatest features, you have a couple of things to consider. The first is the cost of the upgrade itself. Is it really worth the money to get those new features you're eyeing? Another consideration is whether the upgrade will work with your current computer operating system, particularly if you have an older system. Some upgrades may require a newer system to take advantage of the latest bells and whistles, or they may not even work at all.

Using Computer Paper Twice

Computer paper isn't cheap, but you can reuse it by printing on the other side of used paper, particularly if you're just printing off something for personal use. It may help to lightly cross out the used side so you can easily tell the difference between the two. You can also save paper that has been used on one side to use as scratch paper, etc.

Scan All Your Pictures to Disk

Putting all your pictures in digital form will protect them for many years to come, and you can easily and cheaply do it if you own a scanner and a CD burner. Scan all the pictures and organize them by folder (year, event, etc.), and then burn them to CDs, making sure to label the CDs so you can more easily find pictures when you want them. Burn multiple copies to give as gifts to other family members. Your family will love to get their "memory disks," and you'll have copies in the hands (and screens) of others that will be saved and cherished for many generations.

Fill Your Own Ink Cartridges

Computer printer manufacturers make most of their money these days not through printer sales, but through the ink or toner they sell you to use in your printer. Items like inkjet printer cartridges can run you twenty to thirty dollars or more, but there is a way that you can significantly reduce this cost: Refill your own. This requires a little more work, but you'll end up paying half what you would for a new cartridge. Visit the following website for a variety of tips and other information on how to best do this:

http://www.webpanache.com/reprint/refillin.htm

Computers: On or Off When Not In Use?

This is a debate that has been raging in computing circles for years, and you're likely to get a different answer depending on who you ask. On the one hand, computers use electricity, and keeping them on all the time can add up to a couple of hundred dollars of wasted electricity over the course of a year. On the other hand, many argue that constantly turning the computer on and off can wear out its components, costing you far more than you'd pay in wasted electricity over time. The latter argument has lost a lot of validity as computers have become more sophisticated and durable. A great comparison can be found in your television set. If you only watch an hour of TV daily, do you still keep it on twenty-four hours a day? Computers and televisions share many of the same components, and turning a TV on and off doesn't appear to have a huge detrimental effect on it. Neither will turning a computer on and off.

Make Your Own Greeting Cards

Use your computer to make greeting cards of all kinds. Many new systems already-installed software that will allow you to make birthday, get-well, holiday, and other types of cards. If your computer does not have such software, pay a visit to sites such as FreewareFiles.com (http://www.freewarefiles.com/) or Freeware Home (http://www.freewarehome.com/) and do a search for "greeting card." These sites are also a great resource for many kinds of other software.

Make Your Own Calendars

How much did you spend for your last calendar? $10? $25? And, how many calendars do you end up buying every year? You can save yourself a sizable amount of money by printing your own calendars. Your computer may have come with a program allowing you to do this. If not, visit one of the sites mentioned in the previous tip and do a search for "calendar."

Find Cheap Internet Access

We fondly remember the days when free Internet access was starting to take off, and we dreamed of the day when the Internet would be completely free. Of course, the whole movement crashed along with the Internet stocks bubble. You can still find some less expensive Internet access options out there, however. Both Juno (http://www.juno.com) and NetZero (http://www.netzero.com) offer inexpensive Internet access. Other lower-priced (and sometimes free, although these may come with considerable strings attached) ISPs can be found through sites such as Internet 4 Free (http://www.internet4free.net).

Internet Phone Directories, Not Directory Assistance

Don't pay directory assistance to find a number you need. There are a number of free Internet phone directories available online. A great many of them are listed by the Internet Public Library: http://www.ipl.org/div/subject/browse/rcf80.00.00/

You can still find some less expensive Internet access options out there, however. Both Juno (http://www.juno.com) and NetZero (http://www.netzero.com) offer inexpensive Internet access. Other lower-priced (and sometimes free, although these may come with considerable strings attached) ISPs can be found through sites such as Internet 4 Free (http://www.internet4free.net).

Coupons Online

The Internet is becoming a hotbed for coupons, and you can find any number of print-and-use coupons in the areas of bath and body products, food, cleaning supplies, and much more. The following sites are some of the best sources for coupons (many of these sites may require that you register for free to use them):

http://www.couponsurfer.com/
http://www.coolsavings.com/
http://www.valpak.com/
http://www.dealcatcher.com/
http://www.hotcoupons.com/
http://www.couponmountain.com/

Do Your Stock Trading Online

If you like to dabble in the stock market, look into an online brokerage. Online brokerages have reached the point where they offer many services: low trading fees, support, and a wealth of research materials so that you can understand not only how general financial systems work, but can also learn much about individual companies. Other sites such as Yahoo! Finance (http://finance.yahoo.com/) offer many research options for those researching individual companies.

Why Call? E-mail!

Try using e-mail to converse with distant friends and family members instead of calling them. You'll save a lot of money, and you'll have access to additional perks, like the ability to enclose digital pictures.

Toss the Phone In Favor of the Instant Messenger

Talk your friends into signing up for online instant messenger systems such as Yahoo! Messenger (http://messenger.yahoo.com/) or MSN Messenger (http://messenger.msn.com/). These have voice and even web cam capabilities, saving you considerably in phone bills (and giving you the added dimension of video, if you have a web cam).

Send an E-Card

If the person you're sending a birthday, holiday, or other card to has a computer, consider saving yourself a couple of dollars in card and postage costs by sending an e-card. There are many sites online that offer a choice of cards covering every card-giving situation imaginable. While many of these sites have gone to a paying/subscription format, you can still find free cards easily enough by typing the words "free e-cards" into your favorite search engine. Two of the larger sites offering free cards include 123Greetings.com (http://www.123greetings.com) and Free E-Cards Online (http://www.free-e-cards-online.com).

Read Your Newspapers or Magazines Online

Forget about subscribing to newspapers or magazines if you have an Internet connection. With few exceptions, all magazines and newspapers have online websites with sizable archives of reading material. The Internet Public Library links to a wide range of newspapers (http://www.ipl.org/div/news/) and magazines (http://www.ipl.org/div/serials/), not to mention a ton of reference materials and other interesting stuff. You could easily save yourself a lot of money this way, and features like instant alerts and customization (i.e., get only the news you want) are more often than not the norm.

Read Books Online for Free

While not everyone's favorite method of reading, those who don't mind wading into a novel or other book via their modem will find thousands of books online for free. Some sites we recommend include:

http://digital.library.upenn.edu/books/
http://www.gutenberg.net/index.shtml
http://www.books-on-line.com/bol/default.cfm
http://www.bibliomania.com/

Print Out Online Coloring Pages

There are a number of sites online offering free coloring pages that will keep your grandkids busy for hours. One method of finding them is to go to your favorite search engine and type in "coloring pages." A recent Google search using this name returned almost 200,000 pages. Another good source that should come as no surprise is Crayola (http://www.crayola.com). It offers a number of coloring-page resources, including a preschooler section targeting letters and numbers.

Food, Cooking & the Kitchen

Everyone has to eat, and it's pretty easy to bust a budget to meet this need. As such, this is a major area where you can realize significant savings with a little effort. Knowing how to properly store food, how to frugally cook it, and what strategies to utilize when buying it in the first place can pay off immediately in realized savings. This section also provides tips on using your oven more effectively and a number of ways you can get more for your dollar when eating out.

Other chapters you may wish to browse for related tips include Chapter 7 "Gardening & Yard Maintenance," Chapter 13 "Shopping," and Chapter 14 "Utilities" (where you'll find a number of refrigerator/freezer tips).

The Correct Way to Store Sour Cream, et al.

Items such as cottage cheese, sour cream, and yogurt will stay fresh for a much longer period of time if they are stored upside down. Take care that the lids are on securely, however, or this frugal tip will turn into a frugal mess.

Keep Nuts Fresh

Are you looking for a simple way to store nuts to keep them

fresh longer? Like it does with so many other items, your handy freezer will help to retain nuts' flavor and freshness much longer than other storage methods.

The Correct Way to Store Onions

To keep onions fresh, flavorful, and long-lasting, try storing them individually wrapped in newspapers in a cool, dark place. While ordinary onions probably won't gain much from this storage method, flavorful and highly-prized ones like Vidalias certainly will.

Onion Storage II

Another great way to store onions in the kitchen is with something you probably throw away on a regular basis: pantyhose! Place an onion in the hose, tie a knot, add an onion, tie a knot, repeat. The hose will allow air to get to the onions, making them last longer. To use individual onions, simply cut the hose section by section just below each knot.

Consider a Freezer Inventory

A deep freezer can quickly take on the appearance of a dark, uncharted rain forest (or arctic cave, I suppose). You can make much better use of your freezer, keep foods from going bad, and plan meals directly from the freezer by keeping a freezer inventory. Even a

 To keep onions fresh, flavorful, and long-lasting, try storing them individually wrapped in newspapers in a cool, dark place. While ordinary onions probably won't gain much from this storage method, flavorful and highly-prized ones like Vidalias certainly will.

simple sheet of paper taped to the top listing the food within, date entered, and other relevant information will work.

Keep Cereal, Chips, and Crackers Fresh

Bags of cereal, chips, crackers, and the like will stay fresh much longer if you keep them sealed between use. And the best way to do this? Use a simple wooden or plastic clothespin.

Honey Storage

The best way to store honey is in a dry location. Honey tends to absorb moisture, which can make it become granulated.

Keep Marshmallows Fresh

There few foods more unappetizing than a marshmallow that has turned hard. To keep them from reaching this state, try storing them in the freezer. Once thawed, they come out just-bought fresh.

Storing Fresh Ginger

Fresh ginger is wonderful in any number of dishes, but how many times have you bought a root only to have it turn green in the refrigerator? You can keep fresh ginger longer by peeling it, wrapping it in plastic wrap, and storing it in the freezer. Anytime you want that fresh ginger taste, you can easily grate the correct amount from your frozen stash.

Best Methods to Store Bread

Bread should be stored at room temperature, or frozen if the due date is fast approaching. Bread should not, however, be stored in the refrigerator, as this will adversely affect the freshness and taste of it.

Plastic Wrapping Small Items

If you find yourself wrapping up small items frequently with clear plastic wrap, consider cutting the roll in half. This will give you two rolls of much narrower wrap and could lead to real savings over time.

Keeping Grapes Fresh

If you plan to store grapes for an extended period of time (longer than two weeks or so), they'll store better if you pour orange juice over them first.

Summer Cooking Strategies

When it comes to summer cooking, try to target your outside grill and microwave as much as possible. Not only will you save on electricity, but you'll also benefit by not adding additional heat to the house.

Let Cooking Water Cool Before Discarding It

To capture all the heat you possibly can from the kitchen, let hot cooking water cool completely before dumping it down the sink. This will also add humidity to your house, a very important thing in the winter.

How Best To Cook Frozen Foods

Before cooking frozen foods, make sure they are completely defrosted. Not only will they cook more evenly, but you'll also save a lot of energy in the process.

Correct for Excessive Salt Use in Dishes

We've all been there: The soup or stew you're cooking is coming along great, when all of a sudden you get a heavy hand with the salt shaker. Ruined? Not at all! To correct for excessive salt use, try dropping a peeled potato into the cooking pot. The potato will absorb the excess salt as it cooks. Just remember to remove the potato before serving the dish.

Cooking Once a Month

Here's an idea you might want to try to save money on your monthly food bill and save you a ton of time. Get a bunch of friends together each month and have everyone pitch in shopping, cooking, and cleaning up. By the end of the day everyone involved will have a sizable batch of ready-to-heat-and-eat foods in their freezers, and the rest of your month will involve much less hassle and time spent cooking.

Top Secret Recipes

Wish you could make some of your favorite processed or "fast" foods in your own kitchen? Stop by the Top Secret Recipes Website

Here's an idea you might want to try to save money on your monthly food bill and save you a ton of time. Get a bunch of friends together each month and have everyone pitch in shopping, cooking, and cleaning up. By the end of the day everyone involved will have a sizable batch of ready-to-heat-and-eat foods in their freezers, and the rest of your month will involve much less hassle and time spent cooking.

(http://www.topsecretrecipes.com). Top Secret Recipes features dozens of "clone" recipes, from Applebee's® Baked French Onion Soup to Yoo-hoo® Mix-ups. Not only does this offer major kitchen fun, but you'll be able to make your favorites while cutting back on the fats and chemicals that many of them contain.

Using Tea Balls for Spices in Stews

Stews and other dishes sometimes call for spices to be tied up in cheesecloth and then added. If you don't have cheesecloth (or better yet, don't want to incur the cost of using cheesecloth every time), try using a tea ball. Even if you have to buy one, it will come in handy, is cheap and can be reused over and over at no additional cost.

Retaining Vitamin/Mineral Content in Foods

To prevent vitamin and mineral loss in foods, cook them slowly and do not overcook them.

Uses for Empty Butter/Margarine Wrappers

Don't throw away those empty margarine or butter wrappers just yet. Store them in the refrigerator to use the next time you want to grease a cake or bread pan. One to two wrappers will take care of a bread pan, while three should be enough to grease a cake pan.

Alternative to Canned Broth

When recipes call for beef, chicken, vegetable, or other broths/stocks, try to use a low-salt base or bullion cube instead of the canned broths you find at the supermarket. While you'll save a lot of money doing this, definitely keep an eye on the labels, for some bullion cubes contain a sizable amount of sodium.

Sources of Free Recipes

One excellent source for free recipes is your local library. Check out cookbooks and write down any recipes that appeal to you in a notebook or three-ring binder (the latter will allow you to organize them better). This way you'll end up with your own free cookbook with the added bonus that, since you handpicked them, you'll enjoy them all.

Getting Peanut Butter and Shortening Out of Measuring Cups

Peanut butter and shortening in a measuring cup can be wasteful and difficult to remove. You can remedy this by first wetting the cup with whatever liquid the recipe calls for. Using this method, sticky ingredients will easily slide out.

Rescuing Overbaked Cakes

Leave a cake in the oven a bit too long? Overbaked cakes can be easily "rescued" by drizzling a combination of sugar syrup and some form of liqueur (brandy, Grand Marnier, Kahlua, etc.) over them. To avoid such rescues in the future, invest in a good, inexpensive timer. It'll prove very handy and pay for itself in no time!

Keep the Kneading Mess Down

Kneading your dough on a countertop works, but it can create quite the wasteful mess. A better way is to make the dough in a large bowl and kneed it right in the bowl. You won't make a mess, and the whole process is mobile if you want to take it out on the porch or in by the TV while kneading.

When to Buy Baking Staples

The holiday season is the perfect time to stock up on baking staples such as flour or sugar. You can generally find such items very cheaply around Thanksgiving and Christmas (when baking is seemingly required by law), and you can stock up on them for the entire year at a considerably reduced cost.

Fresh Versus Powered Milk

When baking or cooking recipes call for milk, don't use the fresh variety. You can save money by using powdered milk on these instances and save the fresh stuff for drinking.

Make Your Own Spice Mixes

If you've bought any spice or herb mixes lately, you know that you can end up paying top dollar for a little bottle. A much better idea is to purchase spices and herbs in bulk and make your own mixtures. Kept in a cupboard out of direct sunlight, spice and herb mixtures are long lasting and cost a fraction of store-bought blends. If you need recipes for your favorite blend, try entering it into an Internet search engine such as Google.

When Possible, Thaw Foods in the Refrigerator

While it certainly is possible to thaw foods in a microwave if you're pressed for time, you'll save a lot of money by consistently thawing foods in the refrigerator. Defrosting foods, such as meats, in the refrigerator is also much safer than defrosting them on the counter.

Cut Down on Wasted Coffee/Tea Throughout the Day

If you like to drink coffee (or tea) throughout the day, but are sick of making pots only to toss them when they go bitter or cold, consider using a thermos to store the leftover coffee in. You'll always have a fresh, hot cup, and you'll save a lot of money over time by cutting down on waste.

Stretching Frozen/Concentrated Juices

Experiment with frozen/concentrated juices when you add water to them. Usually you can add more water than is called for with little or no degradation of taste. Since this will vary brand to brand, it's best to start with a low amount of water and gradually increase it until a difference is noted.

Salmon Substitutes

If you're dying to try a recipe calling for canned salmon but have been put off by the cost, try substituting canned tuna or mackerel. All three are from the same seafood family and the taste will be quite similar.

Self-Dried Snacks

Consider investing in a food dehydrator. You can make any number of healthy treats (you never know what they put in packaged snacks), and a dehydrator will generally create them much more cheaply than you'd pay for them at a store. This also makes for a great family activity!

Don't Throw Away Bananas!

Are your bananas turning a little brown? Don't throw them away! Bananas can be peeled and stored in the freezer for use later in recipes such as banana bread or muffins. To make them easier to use straight from the freezer, you can microwave them for several seconds to soften them up.

Freeze and Reclaim Small Bits of Veggies

Go through your refrigerator on a regular basis and freeze small amounts of leftover vegetables before they go bad. These bits, cooked and finely chopped, can be used in a great many dishes, including salads, soups, pizzas, casseroles, and omelets.

Uses for Stale Bread (Trash Not One Slice!)

Don't toss away stale bread… it works great to make French toast, crumbs, croutons, strata, bread pudding, bread salad, and many other dishes. Try using it to make Italian bread soup.

Eat Foods "In Season"

Eat "in season." Like Christmas, strawberries, and asparagus should be enjoyed to the point of sickness only once a year. Foods consumed out of season are shipped thousands of miles to reach you, boosting their cost considerably. Be aware of when things come into season in your area and enjoy them then to their fullest. This is also the time to buy these food items in bulk and freeze, can, dry, or preserve them in some other way.

How To Buy Herbs

Have you priced some of those tiny glass bottles of herbs in the store lately? To save money on herbs, buy them in bulk. You can save an enormous amount of money this way. If you're having trouble finding a good supply of bulk herbs locally, try the Internet. Sites like the Atlantic Spice Co. (http://www.atlanticspice.com/) offer bulk spices, teas, and other products at great prices. Another alternative is to grow and dry your own.

Get More Juice from Your Citrus

To get the most juice out of your lemons, limes, or oranges, bring them to room temperature and roll them along the kitchen counter with your palm. You'll want to apply enough pressure to burst the juice cells in the fruit, but not enough to split the fruits themselves.

Leftover-Targeting Recipes Are Particularly Valuable

When browsing through recipes, keep an eye open for those that target leftovers that you find yourself having frequently and wondering what to do with.

Rescuing Rock-Hard Raisins

Raisins and currants that turn into the consistency of little rocks can easily be "rescued" by covering them with cold water in a pan, bringing the water to a boil, then shutting off the heat and letting them stand for five minutes. Just drain and cool them and they are ready for use.

Meatloaf Additions

Many things can be added to a meatloaf to "stretch" it more. Additions such as oatmeal, cooked rice (or other grains), or vegetables not only make the meatloaf more cost-effective but also more nutritious.

Uses for Lemons

Leftover lemon halves shouldn't be allowed to rot in the refrigerator. A better alternative is to chop them into wedges and place them in the freezer. From here they can be used in many ways. One way is to use them as ice cubes in drinks. You can also use them to get rid of kitchen or microwave smells such as fish. Just boil several lemon wedges for a few minutes on the stove (or cook several wedges in a little water for a few minutes in the microwave) and rank smells will be replaced with the refreshing aroma of citrus.

Rescuing Used Cooking Oil

You may feel that oil that has been used to cook fish or other foods is no longer useful due to the strong taste it takes on. You can remove this taste simply by cooking potatoes in it.

Leftover Storage Idea

Next time you're at the store, pick up some of those plastic food storage containers that are divided into sections. Whenever you have leftovers that you want to freeze, place them in individual sections of the containers until you eventually end up with a complete meal. For example, leftover lasagna? Add one serving to each container. If you have leftover broccoli the next day, add a serving to another section of the containers. And on and on until you have a handy collection of homemade "TV dinners" ready to go.

Just boil several lemon wedges for a few minutes on the stove (or cook several wedges in a little water for a few minutes in the microwave) and rank smells will be replaced with the refreshing aroma of citrus.

Making Full Use of Stocks and Gravies

Unused gravy or stock should never be thrown away! Pour any leftover amounts into an ice cube tray, and when the gravy/stock is frozen, pop out the cubes and store them in an airtight plastic bag.

Throwing a Party? Plan Early for Ice

If you're going to have a party, you're going to need a lot of ice. Instead of buying bags of it, plan ahead and start making ice a couple of weeks before the party and storing it in plastic bags in your deep freezer.

Buying & Keeping Cheese

Cheese is not only cheaper to buy in bulk to slice or shred on your own, it also keeps better in large blocks. Still, if you buy it in large enough quantities, you may have a hard time using it up before it starts to get fuzzy. Freezer to the rescue! Most hard cheeses freeze very well, particularly if shredded and stored in airtight bags, and shredded cheese directly from the freezer will save you quite a bit of time in terms of both food prep and cleanup. If you add a little flour to the cheese before placing it in the freezer, it'll help keep the cheese from clumping up.

Make Your Own Superfine Sugar

Don't spend the money to buy superfine sugar. You can make your own by placing regular granulated sugar into a food processor or blender and processing it until you reach the desired consistency.

Save by Eating Less Meat

Try incorporating a meat substitute into a couple of meals a week (or go completely meatless for a meal or two). By and large, meat makes up the bulk of the cost of meals, and you'll find yourself saving money by eating less of it. You'll also be eating a lot healthier.

A Use for Small Amounts of Juice

If you have only a little bit of juice or iced tea left in the pitcher, try freezing it in an ice cube tray. It beats pouring the juice or tea down the drain, and you have the added benefit of chilling future glasses of juice or tea without watering them down if you were to use regular ice cubes.

Saving Bacon Grease

Next time you cook bacon, consider saving the grease that remains. Many recipes call specifically for bacon grease instead of oil or butter, and you can easily save the grease by letting it cool, but not solidify, and then pouring it into an ice cube tray. Once frozen, the "grease cubes" can be removed from the tray and stored in the freezer in an airtight freezer bag. Any time you get a recipe calling for a little bacon (or specifically calling for bacon grease), pop one of these cubes out of the freezer and into the dish.

Reviving Stale Crackers

Crackers that have gone stale can be rejuvenated by spreading them on a baking sheet and then baking them in a 300 degree oven for five minutes. Let them cool completely before storing them in an airtight container or bag.

Never Shop on an Empty Stomach

When food shopping, one of the absolute worst things you can do is walk into the grocery store on an empty stomach. Always shop for food after eating a sizable meal, or you'll face the possibility of rampant impulse buying.

Planning Meals with Weekly Circulars

Plan out your meals the same day that you get the sales circulars from local stores. This way you'll only buy what you need and you will be more apt to use the enclosed coupons.

Buying Meats in Bulk

When it comes to purchasing meats like hamburger and chicken, always buy it in the largest sized packages you can find. Buying meats in bulk is always much cheaper per pound, and you can easily divide the package up and freeze it for future uses.

Is It Worth Paying More For Roaster Chickens?

When shopping for chickens, don't automatically pay more per pound for a roasting chicken than you would for a fryer. A roasting chicken is essentially just a big fryer. You'll save money selecting a large fryer.

Buy Meat "In Season"

If you own a deep freeze, you can save a substantial amount of money by buying meats "in season." For example, just before Thanks-

When it comes to purchasing meats like hamburger and chicken, always buy it in the largest sized packages you can find. Buying meats in bulk is always much cheaper per pound, and you can easily divide the package up and freeze it for future uses.

giving, the price of turkeys plummet, many times to the point where you can pick one up for free if you spend enough money at a given supermarket. Other times of the year where you can get real bargains on meats, include:

- corned beef around St. Patrick's Day
- hot dogs/hamburger around the 4th of July (in the United States)
- ham around Christmas and Easter

See Chapter 13 for much more on seasonal shopping.

Grocery Store Strategy

Visit the grocery store as little as possible, and when you do go, make sure you're clutching a detailed and meticulous list that you swear to stick to. Your list should be compiled at home with that week's sales circulars and your pile of coupons at your side. Make sure you carefully check your refrigerator and cabinets to verify that things on the list are not already sitting on your shelves.

Keep a Price Book

One of the major keys to saving at the grocery store is to know the usual prices of items, and you can best do this by keeping a price book. A price book is simply a small notebook that you use to record the different prices of products at the different stores you hit every week. Note the product and its price at each store. Writing down the date that you recorded the price can also be useful. The price book can be an ongoing project that you always carry with you to the store, and you can add to it a little at a time so that it doesn't become overwhelming. You'll be surprised how quickly it grows and how useful it becomes.

A Month of Chicken in Every Freezer

Find a great sale price for chicken? Buy as much as you can, boil it all up, and then "pull" the meat from the bones and store it in small amounts in the freezer. It'll last for months, and you'll have inexpensive meat on hand to add to a variety of dishes or stews.

Sliced Meats & Cheeses

You can save yourself a lot of money by buying unsliced meats and cheeses and slicing them yourself.

Coupon Tips

Coupons are great, but they aren't the be-all and end-all. If you wouldn't ordinarily buy a product, using a coupon to do so isn't going to save you anything. Also be wary of coupons for products that are sold more for their name-brand than their content. Such things are usually priced well over more generic versions of the same item, and not even a generous coupon will change that.

Cereal Compromise

Your grandkids want the high-priced, high-sugar brand name cereals for breakfast. You prefer to feed them the lower-priced, higher nutrition varieties. Compromise by buying both and mixing them.

Shop Alone

If it can be avoided, try to grocery shop without children. Children have a way of pressuring you into purchasing un-needed items.

Toss the Garbage Disposal

Get rid of your garbage disposal. Not only does it use power needlessly, but you should be using your vegetable food scraps as compost for your garden. Plus, if you have a septic system, constantly running food scraps into it, even through a disposal, isn't a good idea.

Keep Oven Burner Splash Guards Clean

To keep the surface of your stove working as efficiently as possible, keep the metal splash guards under the burners as clean as possible. Clean splash guards will reflect heat upwards toward the pot or pan, while blackened ones will absorb the heat.

Cover Those Pans to Save Energy

Always use a cover when cooking something. Uncovered pans can use up to three times the energy as a covered pan to cook the same foods. Better yet, consider using a pressure cooker. This uses much less energy than traditional pans and cooks food in a fraction of the time.

Match the Pot to the Roast

When cooking anything, try to match the size of the pan or pot you use to what is being cooked. Using a too-large pot or pan wastes energy and increases cooking time.

Turning on the Stove? Fill It Up!

Plan ahead to use your stove to cook more than one thing at a time. Heating it for one item is a waste, but adding a second roast, potatoes, or a pie will make more effective use of the stove's heat.

Stove Alternatives Can Save Money

When it comes to cooking, your stove isn't the only, and certainly not the most efficient, game in town. Appliances like microwaves and crockpots have obvious advantages in the summer time (i.e., they produce a lot less heat), but they also tend to save a lot in terms of money. A really efficient microwave can use fifty percent less energy than a conventional oven, while a crockpot can cook a whole meal for roughly seventeen cents worth of electricity!

Electric Stove Strategy

Do you cook with an electric stove? Unlike a gas range, electric stoves work through the use of heated elements, elements that tend to cool quite slowly after you cut power to them. You can use this to your advantage by shutting off the stove (or stovetop burner) several minutes before the food is scheduled to be done. The elements will start to cool, but still be hot enough to finish cooking your food.

When (Not) to Preheat the Oven

Preheating your oven is a requirement for baking, but that is really the only time you need to preheat it. Foods that are broiled or roasted can be added to a cold oven, although you may have to adjust the cooking time by a few minutes, accordingly.

Your Oven Has a Window for a Reason

As tempting as it may be, don't open the oven door to check on whatever you are cooking. Opening the door will lower the temperature inside the oven by 25 degrees or more. If you really have to peek, turn the oven light on and use the window.

Make Your Own Pot Scrubbers

Hold onto the net bags from vegetables, like onions, to create your very own pot scrubbers. You can do this by simply folding the bags inside themselves and then tying them in strategic places using strong string, fishing line, or dental floss.

Rejuvenate Sponges

Are your kitchen sponges getting a bit nasty? Don't throw them away. Sponges can easily be washed in the dishwasher, which will help to deodorize and sanitize them.

It's Not Garbage, It's Storage

Just about everything that comes through your kitchen is packaged in some manner. Instead of throwing all that packaging away, try to come up with unique ways to reuse it. Old TV dinner trays can be used to heat food in the microwave. Milk jugs can be cut and used as funnels. Smaller plastic bottles make nice starter pots for the garden. Pickle, baby food, and other jars can be used to store anything from nails to buttons. Coffee and sour cream lids can be used on the stove for spoon rests, or as separators when you make hamburger patties and freeze them. Take a good look at something before you toss it and use your imagination to come up with ways it could serve a better purpose than simply taking up landfill space.

Dining Out with Children

Dining out with the grandchildren in tow? Make sure that you target those restaurants that offer free or reduced children's menus. You can easily determine this by calling ahead.

Surviving Expensive Restaurants

Dinners at top-shelf restaurants can be very expensive, but you can still enjoy them…by going at lunchtime. You'll find all the ambiance and many of the same menu items at much lower prices.

Birthday Boys/Girls Eat for Free

Taking someone out to eat for his or her birthday? Check ahead with restaurants. Many will let the birthday boy/girl eat for free so long as there is an accompanying paying customer.

Sucking the Fun Out of Eating Out (While also Saving Money)

If you're eating out, try to avoid both alcoholic drinks and desserts. Both have very high markups and add considerably to the bill.

7

Gardening & Yard Maintenance

Whether you're managing a massive plot in your backyard or a handful of pots on your patio, there are fewer activities more frugal, or more satisfying, than gardening. In addition to providing you with fresh, healthy produce that costs little more than the labor you put into it, gardening is also a wonderful way to relieve stress. Shouldn't you be getting your hands a little dirty today?

The following tips cover all aspects of frugal gardening, from seeds and tools to watering strategies and pest control.

Starting Plants from Seeds Is a Plus

Starting plants and flowers from seeds will save you an enormous amount of money over buying nursery plants and it will give you something to do in the dwindling months of winter and early spring when the urge to garden starts to stray into withdrawal territory. You can save even more by getting together with a friend or neighbor and splitting the cost of the seeds. Usually a packet will contain many more seeds than you could reasonably use in two or three seasons! This is also a great way to experiment with a wide variety of plant types, as the selection of seeds available to you will be much vaster than the selection of plants a nursery can offer.

Grow Your Own Seeds

Try to set aside a small portion of each crop you grow to use for next year's seeds. Select the healthiest plant or vegetable and mark it with a string. When it comes time for harvesting, remove the seeds and dry them before storing them in a cool, dry place. Next year, voila! Free seeds. This works particularly well for vegetables such as squash, pumpkins, cucumbers, and tomatoes. You can also coax vegetables, such as radishes, to develop seeds by letting them grow long past the point when you would usually pick them.

Free Seed Storage Solution

Looking for a cheap way to store seeds saved from the garden? Separate the return envelopes from junk mail and use those. Just make sure to note on the envelope what type of seed each contains, the date harvested, and any other relevant information, and then add the seeds and seal. Seeds should then be stored in a cool, dry place until you're ready to use them.

Check Out Magazines' Seed Swap Sections

Gardening magazines that offer "seed swap" sections are a great way to get free seeds and get rid of those seeds you have no use for. Most magazines that offer these sections will let you participate regardless of whether you are a subscriber or not.

Harvesting Seeds from the Plants of Others

Another source of seeds are the plants and flowers that you see in your neighbors' yards, outside of businesses, or in front of peoples' houses while you're driving down the road. To collect these, wait until midnight, get a flashlight and a fast pair of sneakers... OK, just kidding. Most people won't mind you harvesting some seeds from their plants, but definitely ask first.

Seeds: Hardier than You Might Think

Don't toss seeds at the end of the gardening season thinking they won't sprout the next year. Properly stored, seeds can retain their viability for years. To store seeds over the winter, simply place them in a cool, dry location where they won't be subjected to a wide temperature swing (either too hot or too cold). You can check on the viability of seeds before planting them by placing a few between damp sheets of paper towel. Keep the paper towels moist (but not over-wet), and in a few days you should get a rough idea of what percentage of the seeds will actually end up sprouting in the garden.

When to Buy Bulbs & Seeds

Looking to buy seeds, bulbs, or other plants for the garden? If you can, hold out until the end of the season (planning well ahead to the next season works well here). You'll find that garden centers tend to slash prices considerably at the end of the season.

Save Sprouting Potatoes

If you notice the eyes of some of your potatoes have started sprouting out and gardening season is coming up, set them aside to plant. When you get ready to plant them, simply use a knife to chunk up the potato, one eye to a chunk, and let dry for a few hours or overnight before planting in the garden. Other "sprouters" that can be planted right into the garden include sweet potatoes and garlic.

Using Egg Cartons as Starter Kits

One good use for empty egg cartons: as starter kits for your seeds. If you buy eggs in cartons made with paper fiber as opposed to plastic, you can start the seeds (one or two to an egg depression), keep them watered, and then cut out each egg depression (this should be fairly easy, as the carton should be starting to degrade already) and replant it in a larger container when the plant is big enough. Not only is this an inexpensive solution, but it's also much better for the plants in that you won't be disturbing their fragile root structure.

Make Your Own Sterilized Soil

When starting seedlings in the early spring, it is a good idea to use some form of sterilized soil devoid of bug eggs, weed seeds, and especially fungi that can lead to the dreaded "damping-off disease." You can buy sterilized soil or starting mixture at garden centers, but if you wince at the idea of spending money for dirt, you can also make your own. The Oregon State University Extension Service recommends heating your oven to 250 degrees, lining a pan with soil and then baking it for a half hour. If you have a thermometer, the goal is to raise the temperature of the soil to 180 degrees for a full thirty minutes. Don't overcook the soil, as this can affect its structure. Cool the soil and then use it for your starters.

A Natural Rooting Hormone

To give cuttings a boost when trying to get them to grow roots, try willow branches. Willows manufacture a natural rooting hormone, and if you smash up a few branches with a hammer and add them to the container where your cuttings are, they will greatly help in the formation of roots.

Buying Plants In a Nursery

When buying vegetable or other types of plants in a nursery, don't make the mistake of buying the largest simply because they look great. Smaller ones will cost less and catch up to larger plants in no time, once they hit your garden.

Consider the Cost and Time Necessary for Individual Plants

If you don't have a lot of time or money to maintain plants, steer clear of those that require a lot of both, such as roses. These plants require a lot of attention to maintain and a lot of costly fertilizers, pesticides, etc. to keep healthy and looking good. Before buying a plant at your local nursery (or getting cuttings/root divisions from friends), ask about it or research it to see how "type A" you have to be to keep it thriving and looking beautiful.

Know Your Plants' Likes & Dislikes

Just because a plant looks great in the nursery doesn't mean that it will thrive in your yard or garden. Knowing a plants' likes and dislikes (i.e., the amount of sun it needs, its tolerance to shade, watering needs, soil conditions, etc.) can save you from spending money on plants that won't do well for you. When ordering plants from a mail order catalog or online, make sure that the plant will grow in your "zone." Don't be afraid to ask these questions of the nursery or company you're buying from!

More Vegetables, Less Flowers

Flowers feed the mood; vegetables feed the family. While you shouldn't totally ignore the positive aspects of flowers in a garden, be aware that planting a higher percentage of vegetables to flowers will pay off better (frugal-wise) in the long run.

Think Vertical

If you have big gardening plans but a small gardening space, try thinking vertical. Vegetables such as peas, beans, cucumbers, and squashes can be grown "up" on trellises, existing fencing, or mesh fencing that you can easily erect yourself with a little leftover chicken wire and some poles. This can greatly extend the amount you can grow in a small space, with the added benefit that the produce will be easier to pick (and dirt-free).

Bartering with Your Excess

If you find yourself with an excessive harvest of tomatoes, squashes, or other vegetables that you'll never use, contact your gardening neighbors and see if they are in a similar position with vegetables that you could use. Bartering in this way can greatly increase the variety of vegetables that your garden can help to pull in.

Gardening Clubs Are an Excellent Source for Plants

One excellent source for plants is the sales put on by local gardening clubs. These folks are enthusiasts, meaning that you can often find some very interesting plants, in good health, very cheaply. Keep an eye on the local paper for upcoming sales, or seek out contacts for the clubs and ask if they have upcoming sales scheduled.

Department Store Dumpster Diving

If you have a department store near your house that contains a gardening center, consider driving by their Dumpsters occasionally in search of plants. Many times they will simply toss any plants that are wilted or not selling, as this is more economical than shipping them back to the nursery. This can be a boon for those willing to work with less popular plants or those who are willing to nurse less-than-perfect plants back to health.

Recruit "Volunteers"

Check your garden each spring before you rototill or turn it over to see if you have any "volunteers" you can use for the current year. Volunteer plants are those that self-seed themselves from vegetables that were left behind to rot the previous year. Tomatoes are notorious for self-seeding, and you have the benefit of getting very hardy seedlings that will not need to be hardened off before placed outdoors.

Gardeners' Winter Treat

Winter can be a harsh time for the ardent gardener, but here's one way to keep the growing season alive: Next time you get down to the bottom quarter of an onion or clove of garlic, place it in a pot of dirt in your kitchen. Pretty soon it will develop roots. Even better, it will start to put out green sprouts that you can use in salads, sandwiches, etc. So long as you don't cut the sprout all the way down, you'll have a little indoor garden that will last for weeks.

The Best Way to Store Your Garden Tools

Garden tools can best be stored by keeping the "tool" end in a bucket filled with sand and used oil (cooking, motor, etc.). The sand will help to clean the tools, and the oil will coat them so they will not rust.

Raid the Kitchen for Gardening Tools

Check out your kitchen utensil drawer before heading for the local garden center to stock up on tools. Old spoons, spatulas, large forks, and the like can be recruited for use in the gardening cause to dig, weed, or do any number of other garden chores.

Inexpensive String Trimmer Replacement

Sick of shelling out money for replacement string for your string trimmer/weed whacker? Try low cost alternatives like twine. So long as it is the same width and strength, it should work fine.

Boost Nutrients with a Simple Addition to Plants' Water

One simple thing you can do for your plants to give them a boost of nutrients is to add a little Epsom salts to the watering container. For larger plants, try sprinkling some of the salts directly around the base of the plants.

Boiling Eggs? Set Up Your Houseplants as Well

Give your houseplants an added nutrient boost by saving the water after cooking boiled eggs or unpeeled potatoes and using it as sort of a natural plant food when watering.

Egg Shells in the Garden

Two uses for crushed egg shells in the garden: to keep away snails and to provide extra nutrients to roses.

 Winter can be a harsh time for the ardent gardener, but here's one way to keep the growing season alive: Next time you get down to the bottom quarter of an onion or clove of garlic, place it in a pot of dirt in your kitchen. Pretty soon it will develop roots. Even better, it will start to put out green sprouts that you can use in salads, sandwiches, etc. So long as you don't cut the sprout all the way down, you'll have a little indoor garden that will last for weeks.

Stones for Free

Looking for stones for use in garden beds and other areas of your property? It sounds a little morbid, but check with your local cemetery. They uncover many stones when digging graves and may have a large pile or two lying around for the taking.

Recycle Old Tires for the Garden

A great use for old tires is to stack them in the garden, fill them with dirt, and grow potatoes in them. When it comes time to harvest, little digging is required. Just topple your tire tower and pull the tubers from the resulting pile of dirt.

Do Your Yard Work Personally, or Pay Someone?

How much is your time worth? Do all your own yard work and landscaping yourself unless your time is worth more than what you would pay to have someone else do it. Of course, if you enjoy doing it and find that it is relaxing, this is all the more reason to do it yourself.

Let Your Lawn Be Your Mulch

If your mower is equipped with a grass catcher, you have a cheap and convenient source of mulch. Simply pile the captured clippings around flowers or vegetables to cut down on weeds and the amount of water required. Plus, the clippings will help to enrich the soil.

Use Newspapers in the Garden

One source of cheap mulch to control weeds in your garden is old newspapers. Put down several layers of newspaper around your plants and layer a little mulch or dirt on top them (for aesthetics as much as to hold it down). Try to avoid newspapers with colored ink.

Not only will the newspapers control weeds and retain moisture, they'll also slowly break down and become soil, resulting in a much better solution than the expensive landscaping plastic you can buy.

Possible Source for Wood-Chip Compost

Call your local utility to look into the possibility of getting free wood chips. Utilities work year-round to clear brush and limbs from poles and power lines, and these are invariably ground up in a wood chipper. While the utility may have some form of recycling/composting plan in place for this wealth of wood chips, chances are they will be more than happy to let you have some if you pick it up. It never hurts to ask.

Saving for a Non-Rainy Day

Place containers in areas where you can easily collect rain water (i.e., under eaves or drainage spouts) and ease your water bill when you water your outdoor plants and gardens.

Deep Watering Solution for Gardens

Here's a great solution for getting a lot of water to the roots of plants without wasting it on other sections of the garden that are home to weeds. Poke a few holes into a milk jug and bury it next to the plants. When you fill up the jug, water will seep out and feed even the deepest of roots. You can also add a little plant food to the jugs on occasion to provide an added boost.

Best Time To Water Garden

When is the best time to water your garden? While you may have run into those who warn against doing it at night for fear that the cold, wet plants will be more susceptible to fungal attacks, morning or night waterings are preferable to midday ones. When you water at midday, the sun will evaporate much of the water before it has a chance to reach down to the plants' roots.

Place Thirsty Plants Together

Some plants need a lot more water than others to thrive. You can save on watering by placing these "thirsty" plants together in the garden and then targeting these areas with more water, while using less on areas grouped with plants that require less.

Wash the Car, Water the Lawn

If you wash your car occasionally, don't waste the water you use by letting it run down your driveway. Wash your car on the lawn to make the most out of the water you use.

Find Online Plans for Gardening Do-It-Yourself Projects

From raised beds and arbors to benches and compost bins, Messman's Woodworking Website (http://members.cox.net/messman123/Plan%20Links%20Gs.htm) has links to what must be thousands of do-it-yourself woodworking projects online, including many, many gardening projects. This site is very highly recommended (the above link goes to the "G" page, where you'll find a lot of the gardening projects).

Create Your Own Drip Irrigation System

You can recycle old hoses by turning them into drip irrigation systems for your garden. Just poke small holes into them at regular intervals, and then lay the hoses around the plants in your garden.

Making Your Own Cold Frame

Old windows make cheap and highly effective cold frames, a great boon to any gardener, but particularly those in northern climates. These cold frames can be as elaborate as constructed wooden structures that use hinges on the windows (so that you can easily raise and lower them), to very simple pits where the sides are built up with bricks or stones and the windows are simply then set atop them. Do a search for "build cold frame" in your favorite search engine to find a wide range of plans covering an equally wide range of budgets (or visit the do-it-yourself site mentioned earlier).

Creating Pots Out of Garbage

When it comes to cheap pots for houseplants, seedlings, and other plants, anything that will hold dirt is fair game. These include: milk jugs, laundry detergent containers, plastic soda bottles, etc. Just be sure that you can poke holes in the bottom of these containers for drainage.

Organic Control of Insects

One way you can organically control pests in your garden is to install bird feeders nearby. Not only will the birds eat the seed, but they'll also take a sizable chunk out of the local insect population.

Some plants need a lot more water than others to thrive. You can save on watering by placing these "thirsty" plants together in the garden and then targeting these areas with more water, while using less on areas grouped with plants that require less.

Depending on what you are trying to grow, you may find the birds to be more of a pest than the insects themselves, but this is certainly a low-cost and environmentally safe thing to try in your own garden.

Say Good-Bye to Aphids

To keep aphids off your plants, try a simple soap spray. Combine three tablespoons dish soap with one gallon of water and spray over the vegetation the aphids seem to enjoy.

Aphid-B-Gone, II

Another way to naturally deal with aphids and other garden pests is to plant marigolds around your vegetable garden. The marigolds will help to attract beneficial insects that prey on aphids and similar pests.

Repel Snails & Slugs

One way to keep snails and slugs at bay is to put copper bands around the garden.

Plant a Mosquito Repellent

Looking for a plant that will help to keep mosquitoes at bay? The castor bean plant has long had the reputation for repelling not only mosquitoes, but also flies, moles, and gophers. Be careful if using it though, for it does contain the poison ricin.

Garlic as a Natural Pesticide

One natural pesticide you can try: Crush up a few cloves of garlic and add them to a water bottle equipped with a sprayer attachment. Spray on plants as needed, and keep a close eye on them to judge its effectiveness.

A Natural Mosquito Repellent

Another use for garlic, this time as a mosquito repellent: Roast several cloves of garlic, blend with a little oil, and then add the mixture to your fertilizer dispenser (alternately, garlic powder will also work). Spray this mixture over your lawn, vegetation, etc. The smell will dissipate quickly, but the mosquitoes (and other pests) will stay away. Repeat every two weeks.

Make Your Own Organic Weed Killer

Combine one gallon white vinegar, one cup salt, and one tablespoon dishwashing liquid. Mix all ingredients and transfer to a spray bottle. This mixture allegedly will kill everything you spray it on (well, plant-wise), so be careful when using it around plants and flowers you wish to keep.

Control Grass in Non-Mowable Areas

This may not be something you'd care to try, but it certainly seems to work. To keep grass from growing in those areas near walkways where a lawn mower can't be used, saturate the area with used motor oil.

Gifts

Birthdays, weddings, Christmas, anniversaries, Valentine's Day. It sometimes seems there is no end to the times when we find ourselves needing to give gifts. Not that this is a bad thing! Gifts are our expression of love and appreciation for a person on a special occasion, and we feel better inside when giving them (receiving them is also fun). All these gifts can add up in a hurry, though, and that's where this chapter can help. From general gift-giving tips to specific gifts that you can make, inexpensively buy, and in some cases pull together with just the currency of your own imagination, the following ideas can help you save money while giving gifts that will be enjoyed and cherished.

Only Give Gifts to Close Friends and Family

Don't think you have to shop and buy gifts for everyone you know. Keep gift giving to only close friends or family members. If you do feel obligated to give to other people, make up a few batches of festive cookies and place them in a large, decorated mason jar or other container. You can even wrap them in colored cellophane and tie them up with a bit of ribbon and a bow.

Create a Closet "Gifts Box"

One way to save a lot on gifts is to have them on hand before you need them. Set up a "gifts box" in a closet or spare room and keep it stocked with gift possibilities that you find throughout the year at yard sales, clearance sales, discount stores, etc. When you need a gift for an occasion, paw through the box until you find the perfect one. This will also cut out the last minute "gift crunch," where you'll be stressed to find a last-minute gift and be more apt to spend much more money to do so.

Look Locally when Searching for Gifts

Think locally when it comes to presents for far away family and friends. We all have stuff that is grown or produced locally that others will consider a delicacy. For example, we live in Vermont and have ready access to fairly inexpensive maple syrup, something highly prized by (and expensive for) friends and family in places such as California and Arizona. Look to your own town, county, or state for similar products.

Shipping: What to Avoid

Fragile items are obviously ones you might want to reconsider before shipping them as gifts, but there are a couple of other things to consider when shipping gifts that can save you a lot of money. Bulky or heavy gifts can quickly inflate your shipping costs, particularly if you're sending an item across the country. Also, select items that won't require a lot of excess packaging, as this can also add to the cost of the gift.

Try Making Your Own Flavored Vinegars

Try making your own flavored vinegars! If you have an herb

garden, you're already halfway there. All you'll really need besides fresh herbs are vinegars and some nice bottles. You can even use mason jars; the herbs and vinegar inside them will diminish the plainness of the containers, and adding a little bit of ribbon for decoration will also help. Not only is this an inexpensive gift idea, but it will be highly prized by those who like fine foods. It is also something that you can prepare months ahead of time (if you're planning on giving these for Christmas), resulting in less holiday stress.

Flavored Olive Oils

Olive oil, a few sprigs of herbs, and an empty wine bottle are all that are required to create an attractive and useful gift that the cooking enthusiast will love. It's also one that is very easy to make. Place a few sprigs of dried herbs, such as tarragon, thyme, or rosemary, into a clean, dry wine bottle, add olive oil and a cork or spout, and it's done. The bottle can be decorated with ribbon or even painted for an added touch. Note: Make sure any herbs you use are dried, as the water in them can lead to bacterial growth fairly quickly. Avoid adding ingredients, such as garlic or lemon peel, to the oils for the same reason.

Knit Yourself a Gift

Knitting, crocheting, and sewing can all be excellent ways to make something special for someone (without spending a bundle). Among the gift ideas you can make: afghans, mittens, hats, scarves, aprons, dishcloths, pot holders, throws, pillows, and quilts (for that someone *really* special).

Make Your Own Hot Pads

Even if you only have minimal sewing skills, you can easily make your own hot pads. Sew densely woven material into a pocket and fill it with rice or other grains. Sew up the open side of the pocket, and it's done! Make sure you include a small tag instructing the recipient that he or she can use the pad by simply heating it for two to three minutes in a microwave.

Create Your Own Sachets

Sachets are easy to create and make a wonderfully aromatic gift. Sew small bags out of muslin or scraps of cloth and fill them with items such as rose petals, cotton balls, cinnamon sticks, dried orange peel, lavender, etc. Add a few drops of essential or fragrance oil to enhance the scent and either sew the bags up or seal them with a bit of ribbon. Sachets are fantastic when used to scent enclosed spaces such as closets or drawers.

Make Scented Soaps

Scented soaps are another unique gift idea that you can easily and cheaply create at home. Buy bulk glycerin soap, essential oils, and some soap molds at your local craft supply shop. To make the soap, simply melt the glycerin soap, add a few drops of essential oil, and pour the mixture into the molds. When the soaps have hardened, break them out of the molds and package them up in an attractive way. Oils that work particularly well in soaps include lavender or other floral oil, almond, cinnamon, and coconut.

Your Time, Your Gift

Give a gift of your time. You can easily print up "gift certificates" on your computer or by hand that grant the recipient any number of things that you can do, from massages and baby sitting to car washing, raking, or weeding. For spouses, a series of certificates for sharing some special time together (i.e., go on a picnic, take in a movie, take a long walk on the beach) will be an especially big hit. The sky is the limit here in terms of what you can give of yourself, with the added advantage that all are free (and greatly appreciated).

The Gift of Genealogy

Draw up a family genealogy for the gift receiver. There are many inexpensive software products out there to help with this, and you can make a nice presentation by printing the family tree out and framing it.

The Gift of Memories

If you have access to enough high school or college friends of the gift receiver, try rounding them up and making an audio or video tape where each recalls shared memories of their school days together.

Create Your Own Recipe Box/Book

Consider making up a recipe box or book with all your favorite recipes and giving it as a gift. You can also make specialty recipe collections such as herbs, vegetarian, BBQ, crockpot, and other recipe groups. These make a great gift for newlyweds who are just starting out.

Create Your Own Greeting Card Gifts

Create your own custom greeting cards and bundle them with envelopes to give as gifts. Several ways to make these special include: use stamps with card stock; attach dried and pressed flowers to the outside with inspirational messages on the inside; place photographs on the outside to really prove the old adage, "a picture's worth a thousand words."

Use Your Computer to Produce Gifts

With even minimal graphics software you can use your computer to produce a wide range of printed gift ideas. Some suggestions include: calendars, bookmarks, labels, patterns, forms, pictures, recipe booklets, etc. If you're looking for gifts for children, try entering "coloring pages" into your favorite search engine and printing and binding some of the hundreds of pages you'll come across.

Give the Gift of Creativity

Give the gift of creativity. Write the recipient a poem, story, or song. Paint the recipient a special picture of his or her favorite place or home, or frame an original photograph or collage of photos that the recipient will cherish.

Give the Gift of Video (aka, Your Family, Your Cast)

If you have a video camera (or perhaps even a web cam), get your family together and try making a video message to send out to loved ones and friends. Even a simple greeting message will be highly cherished, or you can test your creativity and just go crazy with it.

Personalize Blank Stationary

If you have a talent with a pen or paint brush, consider buying blank note cards or stationary and personalizing them with your own designs. This is also a great idea if you have skills with computer graphics software.

 Give the gift of creativity. Write the recipient a poem, story, or song. Paint the recipient a special picture of his or her favorite place or home, or frame an original photograph or collage of photos that the recipient will cherish.

The Gift Album

If you take a lot of pictures, give the gift of memory by pulling together a photo album or scrapbook of moments special to the gift receiver.

Create Your Own "_____ Of The Month" Club

You can cash in on the popularity of all the "_____ Of The Month" Club concepts by trying your own. Make up your own certificates and set up your loved one with gifts all year long. You can do this with just about anything, although some good ideas include cookies (or other baked goods), movies, coffee, services (i.e., massage, baby-sitting), etc.

Create a Personalized Calendar

A great gift for family members is to buy an inexpensive calendar (or make your own using your computer) and "personalize" it by adding in family members' birthdays, anniversaries, and other special events. You can add personal touches by scattering shared memories throughout the calendar (i.e., "July 4: Remember that year Uncle Bob set the chicken coop on fire with his homemade fireworks display?").

The "Day You Were Born" Scrapbook

This idea can take some time and research to pull together, but it can result in a very unique birthday present that can be created for just a few dollars. Make a note of the person's birth day and year that you're creating this for and head down to your local library (the library should be large enough to have local and regional newspapers going back far enough to cover the person's birth year). Print local and national stories from these publications that happened on the birth day in question. Some other items to target in the papers could include: advertisements, particularly if the prices of items are very low, or the items themselves very strange to this day and age; sports stories, if the birthday person is a sports fan; any other item that may appeal to the recipient. Take all this information home and pull it together into a scrapbook or photo album for a one-of-a-kind present that will be the hit of the party for not only this year, but years to come.

Create an Inspirational Wall Hanging

A meaningful inspirational quote or biblical verse made into a wall hanging can make a very special gift, and there are a number of simple ways to create one. If you have calligraphy skills, this is the perfect project on which to put them to use. A computer can also create a very attractive document that can be used as a wall hanging. Needlework is another excellent way to create a gift of this nature. Finish it up with an inexpensive frame to display your quote/verse.

The "I Love You Because . . ." Jar

Bypassing the wallet and shooting straight for the heart is the "I love you because . . ." jar. Write on individual slips of paper all the things you love and appreciate about the person you're giving the gift to. Place the slips in a jar, which you can decorate with ribbon, paint, etc. This idea also works well in booklet or journal form, with one sentiment to each page.

Framed Invitations

Did you recently attend a wedding? Take the invitation and place it into a nice frame with either the front or inside wording showing. This makes a great gift idea for Christmas, the couple's one-year anniversary . . . even for one of their birthdays.

Gift in a Jar

Jars, whether fancy or otherwise (mason), can be filled with a wide variety of mixes, fancied up with ribbon and recipe cards and given as gifts. Some of the many things you can include in the jars are dry cookie ingredients, coffee mixes, soup mixes, bath salts, spiced wine or cider mix, pancake mixes, etc.

Create a Bath Basket

Create a relaxing bath basket to help relieve stress. Some of the things you can place in the basket include candles, bath soaps or salts, lotions, a bath pillow, a fancy wash cloth for the eyes, and a tape or CD of relaxing music.

Create Your Own Baked Goods Gift Basket

Put your baking apron on and try filling a basket with a variety of cookies or other baked goods. We did this one lean year with a variety of small quick breads that were very well received.

The Italian Pasta Basket

Another idea for gift baskets is to make up an Italian pasta meal basket. Some of the items you can include in this are dry pasta, jarred sauces, olive oil, herb mixtures, wine, recipe cards, slotted spoons... just about anything that has a fairly good (at least a couple of weeks) shelf life.

 Jars, whether fancy or otherwise (mason), can be filled with a wide variety of mixes, fancied up with ribbon and recipe cards and given as gifts.

Other Ethnic-Themed Gift Basket

Is the person you're buying the gift for an avid cook? Consider making an ethnic-themed gift basket filled with inexpensive items that he or she might not normally buy. Some of these themed baskets, and possible items to place within them, include:

- Indian: biryani paste, cinnamon, ghee, pappadums, tamarind
- Mediterranean: extra-virgin olive oil, falafel mix, stuffed grape leaves, sun-dried tomatoes
- Mexican: black olives, cilantro, cumin, salsa, tortillas
- Oriental: 5-spice powder, ginger root, noodles (several different kinds), rice vinegar, shitake mushrooms

For Grandchildren, the Gift that Grows

Start your grandchildren on the path to a responsible financial future by starting a small savings account for them or giving them bonds, or even stocks. These will cost you little, and the children will learn a lot about money by watching these grow over time.

Sewing for Barbie

Do you have a granddaughter who is into Barbie (or some other) dolls? Next time you're at her house, sneak in and get the doll's measurements. You can make a lot of doll clothes out of small pieces of scrap cloth, and the quality will be higher than the ones you'd find in stores.

Gifts for Pets

Consider making your own cookies or treats when giving pet gifts. You can find a variety of recipes for dog, cat, and bird treats in Chapter 12. Similarly, consider giving homemade birdseed suet to those friends and family members who enjoy watching birds from their windows. Recipes for several different kinds of suet can also be found in Chapter 12.

A Gift for the Family Car Nut

A great gift idea for the car enthusiast is a Car Wash Gift Bucket. Head to your local auto place or department store and stock up on stuff like car wax, washing solution, leather or tire sprays, chrome polishes, sponges, a chamois, etc. You could also create your own "free car wash" gift certificate and give a gift of your time. Store these all in a large car-wash bucket, tie with ribbon and bow, et voila!

The Gift of Blank Medium

Is the gift recipient a movie buff, music fan, or computer nut? Consider giving blank VCR tapes, audio tapes, or recordable CDs. These items are very inexpensive and are much appreciated by anyone who is avidly into such things. Similarly, digital camera fanatics would love to receive a blank photo card for their camera. These have come down in price considerably over the past couple of years, but make sure you get the right type of card. If you know the camera type and model number, the staff where you purchase the card can point you in the right direction.

A Year-Long Gift for Hobbyists

If the gift recipient enjoys a particular hobby, such as gardening or model trains, chances are good there is at least one (and usually more) magazine that covers it. Magazine subscriptions generally cost considerably less than what you'd pay buying magazines issue to issue from the newsstand, and this is one inexpensive gift that will keep giving throughout the year.

Give the Gift of Theater

Consider giving movie passes, or contact the theater and see what sort of holiday specials, gift promotions, etc. it offers. Alternatively, give coupons to Blockbuster or another video rental store bundled with bags of specialty popcorn.

Give the Gift of Non-Cooking

Try giving the gift of non-cooking. Cook a week's or month's worth of meals for the recipient. Every time he or she reaches into the freezer to retrieve another meal (and not have to cook it), you'll get a huge thanks.

The Gift of Green (The Other Green)

If your houseplants are getting away from you, consider dividing them or taking cuttings in early mid-autumn and creating a number of gift plants. Decorate the pots or tie ribbons and bows around them to make them special.

The Gift of Green II

If houseplant cuttings aren't an option, you can still give the gift of green by starting seeds in a decorated pot. Herb seeds work great for this, as do small flower seeds such as marigolds. Another option is to "force" spring bulbs such as daffodils, tulips, and crocus. There's

 Is the gift recipient a movie buff, music fan, or computer nut? Consider giving blank VCR tapes, audio tapes, or recordable CDs.

nothing like a couple of pots of blooming flowers in the middle of February to brighten up a winter mood.

Raid Your Garden for Gifts

If you're an avid gardener, you have a ready stock of gifts already on hand (the season permitting). Pull together a basket of fresh vegetables, flowers, or herbs to give to the non-gardener. You can stretch this gift source into the winter months by drying flowers and herbs and using them in any number of ways, from simple arrangements and jarred herbs or teas to more elaborate gifts such as wreaths and potpourri.

Spice Rack in a Box

This idea is very economical if you give a few of them as gifts. Find a store where you can buy culinary herbs and spices in bulk. Some good selections are ones used frequently in cooking, such as basil, poppy seeds, oregano, thyme, cinnamon, and curry powder. Buy several boxes of very small canning jars, the ones normally used for jellies and the like. Fill the jars with individual herbs/spices, being sure to label each one. The jars go back into the boxes, which can then be wrapped up or decorated. You can enhance this gift by including a few of your favorite recipes that use the jarred herbs/spices.

Give Gifts that Encourage Frugality

There are any number of inexpensive gifts you can give that can help the recipient lead a more frugal lifestyle and use less resources. Examples include reusable tote bags, books for creating crafts, cookbooks for leftovers, etc. Look around your house at some of the things you use or do to save money and use these as inspiration!

9
The Holidays

Ah, the holidays . . . or to be more specific, Christmas. More household budgets break during the period between Thanksgiving and New Years than at any other time of the year. More money is spent on cards, wrapping paper, and decorations (not to mention gifts, which were covered in the last chapter) in the United States alone than the entire yearly budget of many sizable countries. The following tips can help you enjoy this holiday season while keeping the January bills "hangover" to a minimum.

Get Some Perspective

Christmas is increasingly all about hype. Merchants start hawking holiday items as early as October these days, and this trickle turns into a deluge by Thanksgiving. Come at this onslaught with a little perspective. Plan carefully on everything, from how you will spend your money to how you will spend your time. Don't give into the latest fad decorations. Don't feel you have to squeeze something into every single moment to enjoy the season. Christmas had humble origins, and tapping into this by spending quality time with family and friends, while limiting the stress and hype, will lead to much more enjoyment and memories that you will long cherish.

Save with the Secret Santa

Consider doing a Christmas gift swap drawing if everyone is tight on funds. Put everyone's names into a hat and have each draw out a name that he or she will be a secret Santa for. Don't let anyone tell the name of his or her recipient (hence, the "secret" part). When you're not buying gifts for everyone, you can concentrate on getting something particularly special for the one person you chose. If you're doing this long distance, consider using a free online tool such as Elfster (http://www.elfster.com).

Create Your Own Christmas Story

Sit down with your family or friends and create your own Christmas book. Have everyone contribute a chapter or two along a rough story line that you collectively decide to go with (or sit down and brainstorm it as a group). It costs nothing, is great fun, and you'll have something that you can come back to years later and really enjoy.

Replace Gifts for Friends with Time

Instead of exchanging gifts among all your friends, pick out a date where you all can get together to do something special, even if it is only going out for a lunch or brunch close to Christmas. The opportunity to get together and relax during this crazy holiday time will be gift enough.

Holiday Camera Tips

Holidays are the perfect time to take a lot of photos, and there are a number of ways that you can take advantage of this and still save money. First, avoid disposable cameras. You will spend a lot less using your own camera. Use faster speed film such as 400 or 800 to reduce flash time and extend your battery life. You can also save by buying 36-exposure rolls of film instead of several 12-exposure rolls.

Explore Other Traditions

Christmas is celebrated in countries around the world, and many of them have much simpler and more frugal traditions than a lot of the commercial frenzy that surrounds the U.S. holiday season. Visit your local library to find books on holiday customs from other countries to both enrich your own celebration and save on your pocketbook.

Put Yourself in the Mood with Caroling

One free and very festive way to celebrate Christmas is to go caroling. Get together with your neighbors, a church group, or just put up a few banners to attract stray holiday warblers, then go house to house singing carols. If you're organizing the thing, go online to print copies of carol lyrics so you'll all be singing the same words (getting everyone in the same key is another matter entirely). Thermoses of cocoa, flashlights, and warm clothing are a must. To make it really special, collect money from listeners to benefit the local homeless shelter.

The Neighbors' Christmas Lights: Free and Festive

Another great way to celebrate Christmas without spending much: Pile into the car and drive around to see the lights. In addition to displays put on by die-hard amateurs, you'll also find many businesses, towns, and local attractions will put on very impressive displays.

Make'in a List … the Day after Christmas

Get an early start on next Christmas… a real early start. Make a list within a week after Christmas for next year. During the year when you shop, keep an eye on the clearance racks and sales with your list in mind. Not only will you get your Christmas shopping done early so you can relax and enjoy the holidays (well, more than you would have if you had a bunch of shopping to do), but you'll also save money in the process.

Stock Up on Candles and Night-Light Bulbs

Since stores stock themselves silly with candles and night-light bulbs during the holiday season, immediately after Christmas is the cheapest time to stock up on them for the entire year.

Trim Your Christmas Card List

Take a close look at your Christmas card list and see if you can't trim it in half. For those you decide not to send a card to this year, you can always use your computer to send an e-card. Check Chapter 5 for online sources for free electronic cards.

Don't Start Shopping for Christmas Cards too Early

While you may be tempted to start early and get your Christmas cards in November or even earlier, you should hold off until at least after Thanksgiving, as you'll usually find cheaper then. Of course, to really save, buy for next year shortly after Christmas!

Recycle Christmas Cards 1

Save all your Christmas cards from the previous year to cut up and use as name tags on presents for the next year. Remove the front of the card that doesn't have any writing on it and then either fold it in half or cut it in any way that makes sense, given the card's design.

Recycle Christmas Cards 2

Another possible use for last year's Christmas cards: Very carefully cut off the front of the card and use it as a Christmas postcard. Treat the blank side as if it were a regular postcard (draw a line down the middle to separate the text and address if you want), post, and send. This will not only save on cards, but also on postage, as postcards are less expensive to send than traditional cards.

Look Carefully through Discount Cards

Cards bought at discount stores can be a great bargain, but definitely look through the bin carefully. While many of these cards are perfectly fine, others can be a little, to be blunt, cheap looking.

The Christmas Call

Save the cost of both the card and postage by placing a holiday call to friends and family, particularly if you have a good calling plan that allows for inexpensive short calls. This is also a much more personable way to wish someone well during the holidays. Just make sure you jot down a few "talking points" to keep the call short.

Cut Down on Wasted Wrapping Paper

If you measure in your mind like I do, you probably end up wasting a lot of wrapping paper when doing up presents. You can limit this waste by getting a piece of string and pre-measuring the length or width of a present, and then using it as a guide when you cut the paper.

Christmas Paper and Ribbon Year-Round

If you take advantage of low prices for Christmas wrapping paper, bows, and ribbons after the holiday, also keep an eye open for solid prints and more generic bows, ribbons, etc. These can be used year-round for birthdays and other gift-giving occasions.

Save those Bows!

Make sure you save all the fancy ribbons and bows from your presents. They don't go bad (so long as they don't get mangled), and you can always make use of them next year.

One Source for Free Holiday Wrapping Paper

One possible source for festive holiday wrapping paper: the Sunday comic section of your local paper. You could make this even more special by only using various editions the favorite comic strip of the intended gift receiver.

The "Treeless" Tree

Do you want a tree but can't afford one? Consider setting up a "treeless" tree by selecting a corner of the room and running lights from a central point near the ceiling down to the floor. Slant the strings so they create a tree shape. Use bits of wire to attach decorations and garland to the strands and scatter empty boxes wrapped as presents underneath it. While it may not be "real," it will definitely be festive and will put you in the holiday spirit.

Invest in a Fake Tree

While it is certainly true that you could buy a real Christmas tree every year (at a cost of $20–40 or more), and real trees are very festive, you'll save a lot over time by investing in an artificial one. Buy it right after Christmas for next year to save the most money. Not only will you save money, but you'll also have a tree that is a lot less flammable than the real deal. For a little more added realism, try spraying it occasionally with a pine scent.

A Small Tree, Made Big

If your heart says large tree, but your wallet says small, you can appease both by creating the illusion of a large tree. Place the small tree on a coffee table or other small table and scatter a variety of wrapped empty boxes around the base of the tree. This will bring the tree up to eye level and give the impression of being a much larger tree than it actually is.

Frugal Christmas Tree "Themes"

Save money decorating your tree this year by trying one of the following frugal themes:

- The Cookie Tree: If you love to bake, the cookie tree is a perfect way to take advantage of that interest. Use Christmas-shaped cookie-cutters to make a variety of seasonal treats that can be hung on the tree. Before baking the cookies, make sure you use a straw to puncture a hole into the top of each so you can run ribbon through them for hanging. A tree laden with decorated cookies is not only festive, but it is also a sugary treat that you can nibble your way through during the holidays.

- The Card Tree: Use your tree as the ultimate rack to display the cards you receive during the season. Simply punch a hole in the corner of each card, insert a bit of ribbon, and start hanging. You can get better stability with your "decorations" if you glue the front and back of the cards together before hanging them.

- The Snowflake Tree: Everyone has memories of folding up pieces of paper and cutting them into snowflakes when they were kids. Tap into these memories to make snowflake decorations for your tree. Make some larger, some smaller (and just like in nature, no two will be quite the same), and hang them "plain" or decorate with glitter, paint, etc. You can add to the effect by adding cotton batting "snow" to the branches or the base of the tree.

- The Western Tree: Look to nature and things you have lying around the house to make a unique Western-themed tree , String jute rope "garland" around the tree, and then decorate it with tied bundles of twigs, strips of birch bark, pine cones, bows or strips of ribbon, cactus shapes cut out of construction paper, and more. This frugal tree is limited only by your imagination.

Buy Smaller Lights

If you're in the market to buy strings of lights for holiday decorating, consider going with the smaller bulb variety. Small bulbs use less energy and give off less heat, making them more frugal, as well as safer. If you simply must have the larger lights, look for those that use 5-watt bulbs instead of the 7- to 10-watt variety (latter are especially popular in older strings) to save up to 30 percent on the energy cost.

Buy Parallel-Wired Lights

When shopping for lights, make sure you get strings that are parallel, not series wired. In series wired strings, when one bulb goes, they all do, making it nightmarish, if not impossible, to save the lights by replacing the one bad bulb. In parallel wired strings, when one bulb goes, it is the only one, making it much easier to find, replace, and then continue to use the lights.

Double the Sparkle of Your Light Strings

You can get double the sparkle from your strings of lights for the same energy cost by weaving tinsel-type garland through the strings before decorating with them.

Limit Light Use

Don't run your Christmas lights – inside or out – all night, during the day, or when you're not there to enjoy them. You can regulate the amount of time your lights are on by using a simple timer to save on energy costs. You also won't have to worry about forgetting to turn them off when you turn in at night.

Pop the Corn, Get the Needle

A nice inexpensive decoration, and a fun activity for grandchildren or the young at heart, is to thread up traditional strings of popcorn to decorate indoors or out (outdoors you'll also be helping the local bird population). Jazz the strings up with the occasional cranberry!

Bring the Outdoors in this Christmas

If you have easy access to the outdoors and pine trees, save on decorations by bringing the outside indoors this holiday season. Pine boughs, cones, and even acorns will add a great seasonal touch to your house without breaking the bank (use a pine spray for a more pronounced aromatic effect). Make sure the trees from which you collect this bounty are on your property or that you have the permission of the property owner before heading out to "harvest" your decorations.

Decorations by Grandchild

Save grandchildren's holiday artwork and crafts for a very special year-to-year decorating theme packed with memories and love.

Frugal Centerpiece Ideas

The table centerpiece is a Christmas staple, but it can also be a pricey one. There are any number of ways that you can create your own holiday centerpiece, a few of which include:

- Wrap small boxes to create a bunch of "presents" that can be attractively stacked in the center of the table.

- Line a wooden bowl with bits of pine boughs or other green material and fill it with winter fruits, spray-painted pine cones, and walnuts (gold, green, red) or whatever else screams holiday at you.

- Assemble a bunch of bare twigs in a vase and place cranberries or bits of ribbon on the end of the branches.

- Make a bowl of potpourri from materials such as cinnamon sticks, cloves, allspice, dried apples or citrus peel (place any fruits in an oven at 150 degrees for three to six hours to dry them), pine cones, pine bough tips, etc. Sprinkle a little pine, orange, or cinnamon oil (or a combination) frequently on the potpourri to give it both a visual and aromatic appeal.

Leisure

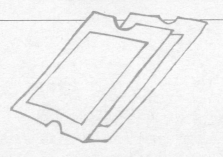

Having fun is important, but it needn't be expensive. The following tips cover low-cost/no-cost activities that you can enjoy either by yourself or with loved ones. Many of these tips are geared toward activities you can do with the grandchildren or others who are young at heart.

Build a Fort

Build a fort in the backyard with your grandkids. If you really want to take it to the next level, research a particular period of time where forts were popular (i.e., the Middle Ages, the Alamo) and regale the little ones with tales of knights or cavalry. Create your own story lines as you storm the gates of the "fort." Serve cookies and milk and set off to storm the neighbor's fort (get the neighbor's permission before you storm his fort).

Bored? Try Board Games

Break out the board games! If you don't have that many, try to borrow or trade with a neighbor or friend. Most families have closets full of games they never use. You can kick it up a notch by hosting a gaming tournament and inviting family and friends. One good way to do this is to find others who have the same game, then run several boards at the same time, gradually working down until you have one winner. Simple prizes will depend on the age, but you can even go with 1st, 2nd, and 3rd place ribbons that you can cheaply purchase or make yourself.

Throw a Treasure Hunt

Create your own treasure hunt for the grandkids. This idea works great at parties! Get a cardboard box that you can have the kids decorate, or try your own hand at it (decorating it to look like a treasure chest would be perfect). Fill it with anything you want, such as candy, small toys, books, pens, or fake "treasure." Hide the box somewhere, then start designing your treasure map. The map should have several areas that the kids have to hit before arriving at the treasure, and you can make it more complicated by scattering clues around, creating poems, etc.

A Puzzling Solution to Boredom

Do you find yourself with a rainy day and nothing to do? Gather everyone together, clean off the dining room table, and break out the jigsaw puzzles. You'd be amazed how addictive and fun these things can be (borrow one from a friend or neighbor if yours are either non-existent or have been put together one-too-many times.

Make and Fly a Kite

Looking for something to do and the wind is blowing? Go fly a kite! Better yet, make your own kite and then go fly it. There are many sites online with plans for building your own kites. To get you started with a simple one, try the following site:

http://www.skratch-pad.com/kites/make.html

Add Water for Fun

When it comes to amusing kids, often all it takes is a little bit of water. Turn on the garden sprinkler or water hose. Have a water balloon fight. You can even entice them into washing the car or their bikes. If it's a hot day, you can't go wrong with water.

Throw a Circus

If you're feeling really energetic, try throwing your own circus. Get the grandkids together and see what tricks they can do. Make a three-ring circus and serve popcorn. Blow up balloons and kick them around. Have Grandpa wear his tux and be the ringmaster. If you have face paint (or can make your own), turn the kids into a troupe of clowns. Dress the family pet up as a "circus animal" (be nice to Rover, though). Expand this by inviting friends and other family members to participate.

Movie Fridays

Make Fridays special by turning them into movie night. Make special kid fare like frozen pizzas, chicken fingers, hamburgers, or nachos, and then check the TV listings to see if there are any good family-oriented movies that the grandkids have yet to see. If not, rent one from the local video store, or plan to buy one on pay-per-view, if you have that option. Pop some popcorn and settle in for a fun night!

Dive In to the Drive-In

Drive-in movie theaters used to be all the rage, and you can still find some of them around, where they offer a very unique viewing experience. If you are lucky enough to have one in your community, keep an eye open for when they are showing family-friendly movies, and then pack up the grandkids, lawn chairs, pillows, and blankets and head out to be entertained under the stars. Bring your own popcorn and other snacks to really save money (food will be a necessity when the dancing hotdogs hit the screen).

Search for Deals at Your Local Theater

Heading out to the theater to watch a movie can be a real treat... a real expensive treat. Call in advance and find out the various prices for ticket during regular/night hours, matinees, etc. Many will also have special reduced admission on a specific night of the week in an attempt to fill seats during a normally dead time. Inquire about this as well.

Kill the Cable

Even with minimal cable, you're probably paying $500 a year in cable fees, and adding any additional channels, especially premium channels, will greatly increase this amount. Get rid of your cable TV and you'll be amazed the time you free up to do more enjoyable things.

Your Library, Your Friend

Do you spend a lot on books, magazines, and newspapers? Stop down to your local library to check out their collection of all three. If your library doesn't have what you're looking for, ask the librarian if it would be possible to get it via interlibrary loan.

Your Library = Free Video Rentals?

Not only can you find books, magazines, and newspapers at the library, but you may also be able to find free video rentals! Ask your librarian if your library stocks videos. And again, if they don't have what you're looking for, ask about the possibility of getting it through interlibrary loan.

Sell Used Books/Magazines to Used Book Stores

Turn already-read magazines and books into extra cash by selling them to bookstores that specialize in used books. With the cash you make, you can purchase more used books from the store. You may qualify for an even better deal if the owner has some sort of a sell-for-credit program in place.

Pay a Visit to Your State's Capitol

Take a drive to visit your state capitol. While what you find there will vary state-to-state, generally you'll be treated to exhibits that lay out the history of the state, guided tours and information, museums, and more, all of which is usually subsidized by the taxpayers (i.e., you've already paid for it, so it's free). This will be a fun and informative trip for the grandkids (don't mention the informative part to them beforehand).

Church: Not Just for Lectures Anymore

Keep an eye on your local church for a wide variety of free/inexpensive activities. Some of the things your church may sponsor include potluck dinners, picnics and other outings, performances, special activities for seniors and singles; depending on the church, the list can be nearly endless. To get even more out of these sorts of activities, offer to volunteer to help.

Tour Everything in Your Area

Look into places in your area that you may be able to tour for free. Such places include factories, fire stations, police stations, radio and television stations, fish hatcheries, wineries, and more. Oftentimes, these places will offer free tours, and perhaps even free souvenirs and refreshments. Call ahead to find out what each facility offers and tour times.

Look to Local Festivities for Fun

Keep an eye on your local newspaper's events listings. Your town, and the surrounding ones, will have a variety of celebrations throughout the year that cost little and offer much. Such things as parades, fairs, historical celebrations, and livestock exhibits all provide a great time for a very little money.

Now Playing . . . in the Park

Your local park is an excellent source of entertainment. Many times you'll be able to find free concerts, plays, and other entertainment events. Contact your town hall (or town clerk) to see if it maintains a calendar of events.

Boost for Local Sports Teams

Check into which local teams are playing. Be it high school, college, local business leagues, Triple A, or the local VFW post, you'll be surprised how many local sports leagues are consistently playing games where you can go and watch for free. Become a fan, cheer loud, and have fun!

Keep an eye on your local newspaper's events listings. Your town, and the surrounding ones, will have a variety of celebrations throughout the year that cost little and offer much. Such things as parades, fairs, historical celebrations, and livestock exhibits all provide a great time for a very little money.

Seek Out Local Organizations

Eagles, Elks, the VFW . . . your area probably has a number of organizations that offer a wide variety of social activities available to those willing to pony up a modest membership fee. Search them out and find out 1) what they charge for membership, and 2) what sorts of activities they sponsor throughout the year. These groups offer a lot of fun and a chance to feel like you are a part of something very special.

Press Flowers

One thing you can do either by yourself or with the grandkids is to press flowers. This can be a very enjoyable hobby that not only gets you outside, but also creates lasting beauty that you can use in a number of craft projects... or just sit around and admire them as winter rages outside. One excellent source for information on pressed flowers that can be found online is Preserved Gardens:

http://www.preservedgardens.com/

Gardening, Family Style

Get the grandchildren interested in gardening early. It is a great family activity that not only costs little, but can also more than pay for itself with fresh and nutritious vegetables. One great way to get kids involved with gardening is to give them their own little plot of dirt to grow whatever they want.

Frequent Farmer's Markets

Keep an eye on your local paper for farmer's markets in your town or in surrounding towns. Many of these offer entertainment and the chance to pick up produce, crafts, and other items very cheaply. It's also a great way to meet and socialize with your neighbors (you know, those people you wave to occasionally as they drive by when you're mowing your lawn).

Pick Your Own

When berries, apples, and other products come into season in your area, pack the grandkids up and head out to pick your own. This is not only a fun family outing (pack a picnic lunch to really make it special), but will also provide you with a wealth of whatever you pick at rock-bottom prices. Make sure that you only pick what you can use, freeze, can, or otherwise store. Some popular pick-your-own crops include blueberries, strawberries, raspberries, apples, corn, and pumpkins.

Hut, Hut... Hike!

Strap on the hiking boots and head for the woods. You don't have to be hardcore about this. Even a simple hike through the local park can be invigorating and fun. To kick it up a notch, seek out the nearest mountain and hike to the summit. Pack a picnic in a backpack and make a day of it!

When berries, apples, and other products come into season in your area, pack the grandkids up and head out to pick your own. This is not only a fun family outing (pack a picnic lunch to really make it special), but will also provide you with a wealth of whatever you pick at rock-bottom prices. Make sure that you only pick what you can use, freeze, can, or otherwise store. Some popular pick-your-own crops include blueberries, strawberries, raspberries, apples, corn, and pumpkins.

Camping in the Great... Backyard

If you have the space, camp for free on your back lawn. This free camping alternative combines many of the great aspects of camping with the luxury of a bathroom and shower close by. Make S'mores, hotdogs, and hamburgers. Sit around a campfire (or perhaps a BBQ grill with a small fire going in it) and stare up at the stars. When you're in your sleeping bag listening to the crickets, you'll soon forget that you're but feet from your house.

Stay with Family and Friends while on Vacation

One way to save on vacations is to target family and friends who live "away" and stay with them. A couple of things to keep in mind with this: Offering to reciprocate and put them up in the future is always a nice quid pro quo and you probably shouldn't target the same family or friends more than once, unless you're really sure they love having you and you are always welcome (as they'll politely say whilst pushing you out the front door). Also be wary of hitting up those family members and friends who live in high tourist areas, such as Nantucket or Orlando. They probably get a lot of such requests, and they may be sick of them.

The Long-Weekend Vacation

Weeklong vacations can get expensive. Why not cut back and go for a long weekend? You may be able to find deals for discounted stays that run three or four days....

Help Yourself by Helping Others

Put your leisure time to good use and come to the aid of a neighbor or family member in need of a good deed. This can include raking, installing storm windows for winter, helping plant spring flower bulbs, shoveling snow… the list is pretty much endless. Not only will you be doing them a favor, but you'll also be feeding your soul. We never feel better than when helping others. Not a bad use of leisure time, indeed.

11

Money: Making It & Managing It

While a chapter on managing money may seem a bit redundant in a book whose whole aim is frugality, the focus of the following tips is much different than what you'll find in other areas of the book. Topics covered in this section include credit cards, insurance, checking and savings accounts, auto loans, home mortgages, and more general tips to help you better hold onto your nest egg.

Keep a Spending Diary

To get a feel for exactly how much you spend every month, keep a spending diary where you write down everything, and I mean everything, that you buy, no matter how small the expense. At the end of the month, go through it and add up all like items to get a good picture of where your money goes. If you do this for several months, modifying your spending as you go, you'll be pleasantly surprised by how much your spending shrinks over time.

Need VERSUS Want

Life is broken down between what you need and what you want. You need clothing; you want $500 boots. You need food; you want a $100 steak dinner at your favorite restaurant. Take some time to factor the difference between what you want and what you need in your life. Being able to see things in this light, and concentrating up on what you need rather than upon what you want, will help cut down on your spending considerably.

Money Before Plans

Here's another great idea when it comes to budgeting: Don't spend money based upon the plans that you make. After you have met your financial obligations, take the remaining money and then make plans according to it.

Do Your Own Taxes

Unless your financial life is hugely complicated, save money by doing your own tax returns. Software, such as TurboTax, is worth its weight in gold for those with difficult returns, small businesses, etc., while those with "simpler" lives can get by without computer-program assistance fairly easily and just do their taxes by hand. Look to the IRS home page (http://www.irs.gov) for forms, publications, and help in filling out the forms, and file on time (or file for an extension) to avoid penalties!

Increase Income or Decrease Spending?

Saving money essentially boils down into two distinct strategies: Either increase the amount of money (income) you bring in, or decrease the amount (spending) that goes out. If you've found that you're always concentrating on one of these options and have had little luck in improving your financial situation, considering switching to the other.

Live within Your (Not Your Friends') Means

It's as old as keeping up with the Joneses, but it's still valid: Don't feel that you have to try and keep up with your friends' spending habits.

Writing off Restaurant Visits

Do you own a business and love to dine out? Combine the two and you have a legitimate write-off for your taxes. Yum.

Shop Around when Opening any Kind of Financial Account

When looking to open any kind of savings, checking, or investment account, make sure that you contact several different institutions to see what each offers, what the fees and penalties are, etc. As you start to shop around, you'll be surprised at how much these can vary.

Check for Insurance (FDIC, NCUA) Before Opening an Account

Before opening any sort of savings or investment account, make sure that the account will be insured by the federal government (FDIC or NCUA). Depending on the institution, many financial prod-

 Unless your financial life is hugely complicated, save money by doing your own tax returns. Software, such as TurboTax, is worth its weight in gold for those with difficult returns, small businesses, etc., while those with "simpler" lives can get by without computer-program assistance fairly easily and just do their taxes by hand.

ucts offered these days, including annuities and mutual stock funds, may not be insured.

Highest Return with the Lowest Risk Investments

What can offer you the highest return with little or no risk? CDs (certificates of deposit) or U.S. savings bonds.

Keep Credit Cards in a Lock Box

Having a credit card for emergency purposes is generally a good idea, but only if that is all it is used for. Avoid using credit cards for general purposes such as shopping. You'll tend to be considerably more frugal watching the cash leave your wallet, or watching the total shrink in your checkbook register.

An Interesting Solution to Credit Card Spending

I recently ran across this humorous suggestion for stopping your credit card spending: Freeze the card in a block of ice. You can do this by filling a plastic container half-full of water, letting it freeze, then adding the card and more water before returning it to the freezer. Take it out every once in a while to renew your commitment to avoiding it.

Leave the Credit Cards at Home

Leave your credit cards at home when you head to the store. You can always go back to get your credit card if you really, really want something and need the credit card to purchase it. At the very least, this will give you a "cooling off" period to think about it. Being forced to pay cash for purchases will also make you think a bit more before cracking out the wallet.

Pay off Your Credit Card Balance each Month

The conventional wisdom holds true: Paying off your credit card balance each month can save you upwards of thousands of dollars a year in interest charges.

Savings or Credit Card: Which to Pay?

It's nice to have money in your savings account, but if you can use it to pay off your credit card, do so. The interest you pay on your card is usually much higher than the interest you make on your savings account, and you'll just be losing money in the long run letting your card run with a balance.

An Alternative to Credit Card Insurance

Is your credit card company spinning tales of gloom and trying to sell you credit card insurance? This is a type of insurance that pays off your debts if something bad happens to you. It sounds nice, but the rates companies charge can be high. Look into term life insurance, which can do the same thing, only cheaper.

Make Your Credit Card Company Pay You

If you really insist on getting and keeping a credit card, try to get something for your troubles. Credit card companies are very competitive, and at the very least, you can try to negotiate for a lower annual percentage rate (APR). Other perks that you can try to get include cash back rewards, phone minutes, free air miles, etc. Don't be afraid to force the credit card companies to go the extra mile to gain your business.

Avoid Credit Card Cash Advances

You probably have the ability to take a cash advance on your credit card, but avoid this if at all possible, particularly if you have another loan avenue open to you. The rates that most credit cards charge for cash advances is considerably higher than what they charge for purchases (which is a high enough rate to start with!).

Buy Only the Insurance You Need

Don't be talked into buying insurance you don't need (i.e., life insurance for children).

Life Insurance Suggestion

Are you looking to buy a whole life, universal life, or other cash value policy? In order to keep your life insurance costs from more than doubling, plan on holding onto these policies for at least 15 years.

When to Raise Your Car Insurance Deductibles

When it comes to car insurance, consider approaching your broker about raising the deductibles on your collision and comprehensive coverage to at least $500. If your vehicle is really old, consider dropping your deductible altogether.

Before Getting Insurance, Visit the NAIC

When it comes to insurance companies, it's always a good idea to check into a company's financial well-being. You can do this at the National Association of Insurance Commissioners' website (http://www.naic.org/cis/). This site also allows you to file consumer complaints.

Shop Around for Auto Loans

When it comes to auto loans, you can save hundreds of dollars in finance charges over the life of the loan by shopping around. Check out several local banks, your credit union, and even possibly the manufacturer's own finance company to see who can offer you the best rate.

Beware of Checking Account Fees

Always look into the various checking charges (ATM/debit card fees, minimum balance requirements, etc.) before signing up for a checking account. Checking accounts with low/no minimum balance requirements can save you considerably in fees over the course of a year.

Consider Direct Deposit

If it is a possibility, definitely consider direct deposit. Not only is this convenient (no lunchtime run to the bank) and secure, but in many cases a bank will give you a bargain when it comes to checking account fees if you also use them for direct deposit. Contact your bank to see what it can offer you in this area.

Bill Yourself to Increase Savings

One innovative way to sock money away every month is to write yourself a bill (everybody else is sending you bills, why not yourself?). Bill yourself every month, pay yourself first, and you'll see your savings grow.

Beware of Adjustable Rate Mortgages

Be weary of adjustable rate mortgage loans (ARMs). The rate of these can vary wildly over the life of the mortgage, which can result in swings of several hundred dollars a month in payments. They may look attractive when you first get one, but there's a lot to be said for the reliable month-to-month payments of a fixed-rate mortgage.

The Home Inspector, Your Best Friend

One thing you do not want to neglect when buying a house: a house inspection. We've worked with an inspector on the last two houses we put bids on (we actually bought the last one), and he was well worth the $300–400 dollars we paid. Not only will an inspector alert you to major problems that will affect your ultimate offer, but he or she will also give you a heads-up on areas you may need to concentrate on five, ten, or even more years into the future. Bottom line: A home inspection will give you a very clear snapshot of the health of your house at the moment of sale.

Consider a Buyer Broker

Would you prefer to have someone on your side when you set out to buy a house? Consider going with a buyer broker. The buyer broker can help you with all aspects of the sale, and he or she can usually get you a better price for the house.

The Consumer Credit Counseling Service

If you feel like you're at the end of your rope financially, there's an organization that is waiting to hear from you. The Consumer Credit Counseling Service offers free credit counseling and a variety of other services to help you financially. Check out its website at http://www.cccsintl.org/.

12
Pets & Animals

Pets are our "four-legged children," and much like children, the cost for their upkeep can quickly add up. This chapter looks at ways that you can save money on everything from home remedies to food and vet bills. If you're feeling really creative, this chapter concludes with a number of recipes for treats that will quickly get the attention of even the most finicky dogs, cats, and birds.

Smaller Is Cheaper

When trying to decide on a pet, remember that, generally speaking, the smaller it is, the less it will cost in the long run. This is particularly true of very small mammals, such as rats, hamsters, rabbits, and guinea pigs, which will not only cost much less than dogs and cats, but will also require less of your time.

Don't Let Frugality Endanger Your Pet

Saving money when it comes to your pets is a great goal, but don't let it be the be-all and end-all. Saving a buck isn't worth endangering your pet.

Keep Dogs from Chasing Cars

Having problems with a dog that chases cars? Try attaching a stick to the dog's collar, so that it strikes its knees when it tries to run.

Make Your Own Pet Toys

That plastic squeaky pork chop at the store may look like the perfect toy for your pet (well, until you have to sit there and listen to it for several hours non-stop), but you can save yourself a few dollars by making your own pet toys. For dogs, anything involving an old sock is a sure hit; place a tennis ball inside one, or tie several together to make a tug toy. Cats will entertain themselves for hours with anything dangling from a string. Cats also enjoy bubbles that you blow (make your own out of a small amount of dish soap and water), or you can sew up a small pouch from scrap cloth and fill it with catnip and cotton. For your feathered friend, some hits include bubble wrap, a little ball hanging from a string, and even something as simple as a rubber band wrapped around its perch to keep it entertained for hours (keep an eye open to make sure your bird doesn't start eating the rubber band).

A Cost-Effective Alternative to Litter?

While the following tip may seem to some to be more like "mucking a barn," it is a possible way to save a considerable amount on litter. Instead of regular litter, try using cedar shavings.

Senior Discounts

Don't forget to inquire about senior discounts at the vet's office, the pet shop, or wherever else you shop for food and other pet supplies.

Pet Freebies Online

Looking for sources for pet freebies online? Consider visiting some of the following websites:

http://www.totallyfreestuff.com/
    index.asp?Level1=Pet+Freebies
http://www.freestuffsearch.com/cat/pet1.html
http://www.bestdealsontheweb.net/pet_freebies.html
http://www.pet-parade.com/freestuff/
http://www.coolfreebielinks.com/Pet_Freebies/
http://www.fabfree.com/pet.htm
http://freebies.about.com/cs/catfreebies/
http://freebies.about.com/cs/dogfreebies/

Do It Yourself Grooming, Clipping, and More

If you're feeling adventurous, you can tackle such pet tasks as nail clipping, grooming, and dental cleaning yourself. Look to your library to rent tapes, purchase your own, or search the Internet for relevant information. These are all things that must be periodically done for pets, and they are all things that can save you a considerable amount of money if you do them yourself.

An Herb that Can Help with Fleas

From the "one more idea to keep fleas off pets" department: Try adding a little sage to their food. Sage can be easily purchased in the herb section of any supermarket, or you can grow your own.

Try Making Your Own Flea Collar

Let's face it: That is poison you're placing around your pet's neck when you put a flea collar the pet. A cheaper and safer solution may be to makeing your own flea collars using essential oils. Rubbing any of the following essential oils into a standard collar every week could help with flea problems (if you don't seem to be seeing any effect, try a different essential oil): eucalyptus, geranium, lavender, or tea tree.

Home Remedy for Dog Skin Allergies

Before giving in and spending high amounts on creams and other medications to treat your dog's skin allergies, try the following home remedy: Cook some comfrey greens in water and, then strain the greens out and allow the "tea" to cool. Pour this onto the dog's fur and massage it into the skin lightly. Since this can be a very powerful concoction, use it only when necessary, and do not use it more than once a month.

Clean Your Dog's Ears on the Cheap

Does your dog suffer from repeated ear infections or irritations? The ear cleaner you buy from the vet or pet store can get pretty expensive, but you can make your own by mixing equal parts rubbing alcohol, white vinegar, and water. Squirt a few drops in to your pet's problem ear, let it sit for a minute or so (you can massage the ear if you want to really do a good cleaning job), and then wipe the mixture out with a tissue.

Let's face it: That is poison you're placing around your pet's neck when you put a flea collar on. A cheaper and safer solution may be to make your own flea collars using essential oils. Rubbing any of the following essential oils into a standard collar every week could help with flea problems (if you don't seem to be seeing any effect, try a different essential oil): eucalyptus, geranium, lavender, or tea tree.

Cure Pet Diarrhea

When it comes to dealing with pet diarrhea, this tip has been making the rounds, and although I haven't tried it myself, it's certainly worth a frugal shot. If your pet has diarrhea, try curing it with a little Gatorade in its bowl.

Pet Carpet Accident Solution

Are your pets peeing on the carpet? One simple solution is to generously douse the area with baking soda, let the area dry, and then vacuum thoroughly. The baking soda will not only take out the stain, but also the odor.

Prevention Can Save Money

Keeping your pet clean and in good health is one of the best ways you can keep it happy and healthy. Your pocketbook will also thank you.

Homemade Skunk Scent Formula

Out of tomato juice and Skipper had a run-in with a skunk? Try mixing the following together and rubbing it into the befouled fur:

- 1 quart hydrogen peroxide
- ½ cup baking soda
- 1 teaspoon liquid soap

Rinse afterward with water to remove this mixture, as well as a considerable amount of the skunky scent.

Vaccinate Your Own Pets?

Did you know that in many states you can administer most of

your pet's shots yourself (except for rabies). This will vary state to state, so definitely check with your state veterinary board to make sure what you can and can't do. Any shots that you are able to administer yourself can be purchased over the Internet at sites such as 1-800-PetMeds (http://www.1800petmeds.com/).

Shop for Vets

Before settling on a vet, call around to check prices for specific procedures. Veterinary prices can vary greatly. Also ask friends and family for get recommendations.

Veterinary Alternatives

Vet bills can run up quickly, but depending on your area you may have some alternatives when it comes to pet care. Call your local humane society to see what services it provide's (and how much it charges), or get in touch with the local university/college to see if it has veterinary programs that offer substantial discounts for pet services.

Check into Spay/Neuter Clinics

Can't afford the cost of spaying or neutering your pet? Check your area for any spay clinics sponsored by local pet shelters or other pet groups. Many areas now feature these clinics, which can save you a sizable amount of money over spaying/neutering your pet at a veterinarian's office.

Track Vet Procedures

Keep a pet log where you write down every shot and other procedure that your pet undergoes while at the vet's office. If at some point in the future you decide to switch vets, all this information will be at your fingertips, and you'll avoid having to pay for duplicate procedures.

Group (Herd?) Discounts

If you have several pets, ask your veterinarian if he offer's group discounts for bringing in more than one pet at a time for routine examinations and shots. Your pets may also experience a lot less "vet anxiety" if surrounded by familiar furry faces.

Stray Savings

Is your pet one that was abandoned or rescued? Mention this to the vet and ask if he offer's discounts for strays.

Shop for Pet Food

Shop for prices when it comes to pet food. Brands of food can vary quite sharply when it comes to price, and often times if you read the ingredients list, there really isn't much difference between them... except for the price.

Where Not to Buy Food

When it comes to food, avoid buying it from the veterinarian. Many of the special diet blends vets try to steer you toward will cost

 Can't afford the cost of spaying or neutering your pet? Check your area for any spay clinics sponsored by local pet shelters or other pet groups. Many areas now feature these clinics, which can save you a sizable amount of money over spaying/neutering your pet at a veterinarian's office..

you a considerable amount more than if you stock up at discount pet superstores. While it is true that some pet's will do better on specialized diets, if your pet is in good health, you're probably just wasting your money buying vet food. The vet, on the other hand, realizes a handy profit for each bag of premium chow that he sell's.

Save on Cat and Dog Food

Here's another tip when it comes to saving money on food for Fido or Fluffy: Check with your local humane society. It often sell's food very cheaply, with the added bonus that the money goes to a good cause.

Buy Pet Food in Bulk

You can save a lot by buying pet food in bulk, but often buying and storing large amounts of food for, say, a Chihuahua, isn't practical. Consider going in with friends or neighbors to buy larger bags of food which can be split.

Pep-up Cheaper Foods

Nutritionally, cheaper pet foods may be similar to more expensive brands, but if your pet is used to eating the "good stuff," it may turn up its nose at first to the cheaper varieties. You can pep-up cheaper foods by including a touch of your own leftovers or pan drippings to the food, but make sure you avoid excess salts or fats.

Canine Flea Biscuits

Garlic has long been known for its ability to control fleas. It's combomed in the following recipe that will make a tasty treat that your dog(s) will love!

- 2 ½ cups whole wheat flour
- ½ cup powdered milk
- 1 teaspoon brown sugar
- ½ teaspoon garlic powder
- 1/3 cup meat drippings
- 1 egg - beaten
- ½ cup ice water

Combine the flour, milk, brown sugar, and garlic powder. Cut the meat drippings into the flour mixture until you form a grainy mixture the size of peas. Beat in the egg, and then slowly beat in the water just to the point at which you can form a ball with the dough. Turn the dough onto a lightly floured surface, roll out to about one-half inch thick, and use your favorite cookie cutter to cut out cookie shapes. Bake on a greased cookie sheet at 350 degrees for 25–30 minutes.

You can store these in the refrigerator (one month) or freezer (one year).

Mint/Parsley Dog-breath Basher Biscuits

Use this recipe to eliminate "puppy breath."

- 2 cups brown rice flour
- 1 tablespoon activated charcoal
- ½ cup chopped fresh parsley
- 1/3 cup chopped fresh mint
- 3 tablespoons vegetable oil
- 1 egg
- 2/3 cup milk

Combine the flour and charcoal in a small bowl. In a larger bowl, combine the parsley, mint, oil, and egg and beat together well. Alternate, adding the dry ingredients to the egg mixture with the milk, stirring well after each addition. Drop the resulting dough by spoon onto a greased cookie sheet, and then bake in a 400 degree oven for 15 minutes. When cool, store in the refrigerator (one month) or freezer (one year).

Chicken Liver Cookies

- 1 cup flour
- 1 cup cornmeal
- 1 egg
- 3 tablespoons vegetable oil
- ½ cup chicken broth
- 2 teaspoons parsley
- 1 cup cooked chicken liver chopped,

Combine the flour and cornmeal in a small bowl and set aside. In a separate bowl, beat the egg and oil, and then add the chicken broth and parsley, mixing well. Stir in the dry ingredients a little at a time until completely incorporated, and then fold in the chicken livers. Roll the dough on to a floured surface into a thickness of one-half inch inch and cut into whatever shapes you choose. Place the cookies on a greased cookie sheet and bake at 400 degrees for about 15 minutes, or until firm. When cool, store in the refrigerator.

Cheesy Dog Treats

- 1 cup boiling water
- 1 cup rolled oats
- 1/3 cup margarine
- 1 cup shredded cheddar cheese
- ¾ cup cornmeal
- ½ cup milk

- 1 egg, beaten
- 1 tablespoon granulated sugar
- 2 teaspoon. chicken or beef bouillon granules
- 2 ½ – 3 cups all-purpose or whole wheat flour

In a large bowl, combine the boiling water, oats, and margarine and allow to set for several minutes. Add the cheese, cornmeal, milk, egg, sugar, and boullion and stir to combine. Add the flour a little at a time, stirring after each addition, until all is incorporated into a dough. Turn the dough onto a lightly floured surface and roll it out to one-half inch thickness (you may need to add a little more flour to it to make it less sticky). Cut out your favorite cookie shapes, then bake on a lightly greased cookie sheet at 325 degrees for 35 to 45 minutes, or until golden brown.

Peanut Butter Puppy Cookies

- 1 package dry yeast
- ½ cup warm water
- 1 cup mashed potatoes
- 1 cup milk
- ¼ cup molasses
- ½ cup chicken broth
- 1 cup peanut butter
- 1 cup wheat flour
- 3 cups white flour
- 1 egg

In a large bowl, combine the yeast and water and allow to dissolve. In a saucepan, mix together the potatoes, milk, molasses, chicken broth, and peanut butter. Bring to a boil, stirring frequently, and then remove the mixture from the heat and let it cool. Add the yeast, and then gradually add the flours and egg. Add as much flour as you need to create a workable ball, and then roll it out to one-half inch thickness on a lightly floured surface. Cut into cookie shapes, and bake on an ungreased baking sheet at 325 degrees for 45 minutes. Cool and serve whenever you wish (these should be fine left out in a canine cookie jar for a couple of weeks).

Tomato/Wheat Dog Biscuits

- ¼ cup hot water
- 8 chicken or beef bouillon cubes
- 1 packet active dry yeast
- 2 cups all-purpose flour
- 2 cups wheat germ
- 1 ½ cups whole wheat flour
- 1 ½ cups tomato juice
- 1 teaspoon granulated sugar

In a large bowl, combine the boullion and the hot water, and then let the mixture sit for a few minutes so it cools a bit. Stir the yeast into the broth and let sit for another five minutes. Stir in the rest of the ingredients until combined, then turn the dough onto a lightly floured surface. Roll the dough out to one-quarter inch thickness and cut into cookie shapes of your choosing. Place the cookies on a greased cookie sheet and bake in a 300 degree oven for one hour. When cool, you can store these in the refrigerator for up to a month or in the freezer for up to a year.

"Vegetarian" Dog Cookies

- 1 cup flour
- 1 cup wheat flour
- ½ cup powdered milk
- ½ cup wheat germ
- 6 tablespoon butter or margarine
- 1 egg
- 1 teaspoon brown sugar
- 1 cup mashed vegetables

Combine the flowers, powered milk, and wheat germ in a bowl. Cut in the butter and work it in until you obtain a consistency similar to small peas. In a separate bowl, cream the egg and sugar together. Add the mashed potatoes and egg mixture to the dry ingredients and mix thoroughly. Roll onto a lightly floured surface and cut with your favorite cookie cutter shape. Place on a lightly greased cookie sheet and bake at 325 until lightly browned.

Catnip Cookies

- 1 cup whole wheat flour
- 2 tablespoons wheat germ
- ¼ cup soy flour
- 1/3 cup confectioners' milk
- 1 tablespoon kelp
- ½ teaspoon bone meal
- 1 teaspoon crushed dried catnip leaves
- 1 tablespoon unsulfured molasses
- 1 egg
- 2 tablespoons oil, butter or fat
- 1/3 cup milk or water

Combine all the dry ingredients, then add all the wet ingredients and mix until you have a workable dough. Roll the dough out flat on to an oiled cookie sheet and cut into thin strips. Bake in a 350 degree oven for about 20 minutes, or until lightly browned. When cool, break the strips into cat-sized bits.

Cat Mackerel Treats

Note: The brewer's yeast in this recipe can help to keep fleas off kitties, as well as provide fatty acids and B vitamins to produce glossy coats and help the feline nervous system.

- ½ cup canned mackerel drained and crumbled
- 1 cup whole grain bread crumbs
- 1 tablespoon vegetable oil
- 1 egg, beaten
- ½ teaspoon brewer's yeast

Combine all ingredients and mix well, then drop by the spoonful onto a greased cookie sheet. Bake in a 350 degree oven for eight minutes. When cool, store in the refrigerator (three weeks) or freezer (one year).

Kitty Tuna Cookies

- 1 cup whole wheat flour
- 6 ounce canned tuna in oil, undrained
- 1 tablespoon vegetable oil
- 1 egg

Combine all ingredients and mix well. Roll out to one-quarter inch thick on a lightly floured surface and cut into cookie shapes. Bake onto an ungreased cookie sheet at 350 degrees for 20 minutes or until firm. When cool, store in the refrigerator (three weeks) or freezer (one year).

Cockatiel/Parrot Food Mix

- 2 cups millet
- 1 cup safflower seeds
- 1 cup buckwheat, wheat-berries, or sunflower seeds
- 2 cups whole oats

Mix all ingredients and store in a cool, dark place in a sealable container. This can be used as your bird's main food source, which can be supplemented with fresh fruits and vegetables daily.

Canary Paste

- ¼ cup almonds
- 2 tablespoons sweet butter, softened
- ¼ cup cornmeal
- 2 tablespoons honey

Process the almonds in a food processor until they reach a fine consistency. Add the cornmeal and process for another minute or so. Cream the butter and honey together in a bowl until combined, and then stir the dry ingredients in until you have a paste. Simply pack the paste into your canary's feeding tray and let the feeding frenzy begin!

Hummingbird Food

- 2 cups water
- ½ cup granulated sugar

Boil the two ingredients until the sugar is entirely dissolved, let cool, and then fill your hummingbird feeder the blend. There is no need to add red food coloring, as your hummingbird feeder should already be red-colored. This mixture will last for up to a week in the feeder (in the shade) before starting to ferment. When you replace it, make sure you clean the feeder well.

Outdoor Bird Balls

- 1 pound of lard
- 1 jar of peanut butter
- 5 cups corn meal
- 6 cups oats
- 2 cups sunflower seeds
- 2 cups raisins

Mix the first four ingredients together, form into balls, and then roll them in the sunflower seeds and raisins. Place the balls outdoor's in a suet cage or bird feeder. This is great for the winter time, when birds need more energy to keep warm.

Peanut Butter Suet

- 1 cup cornmeal
- 1 cup peanut butter
- 1 cup sugar
- ¾ cup flour
- 1 cup water
- 1–3 cups birdseed (depending on the size of the seed; when in doubt, try 2 cups)

Combine all ingredients, except for the birdseed, and microwave for five minutes. Halfway through, stop the microwave and stir thoroughly to combine. Let the mixture cool for a bit after microwaving, and then stir in the seed. When fully cool, shape into blocks that will fit into your suet feeder (or an onion bag) and freeze until needed.

A More Traditional Suet

- 1 ¼ pounds suet
- ½ cup sunflower seeds
- ½ cup crushed peanuts
- ½ cup cracked corn kernels

Melt the suet in an oven or sauce pan, and then stir in the rest of the ingredients. Spoon the mixture into a mold of some kind and insert a drinking straw through the top. Place into the refrigerator to cool. When solid, break the suet out of its mold, remove the straw, and thread a string through the hole that remains. Hang the suet from any limb in the shade (alternately, leave out the straw step and just place the suet into a suet cage).

Coconut Bird Feeder

Here's an interesting alternative to traditional suet feeders. Cut a coconut in half with a hacksaw and remove the meat from both halves. Drill a hole in each half and tie a long string or cord through the hole. For the filling, grate the coconut and combine it with warmed vegetable shortening, lard, or suet (about one part lard to two parts grated coconut). Fill the cups and hang outside in the shade.

13
Shopping

Let's face it, shopping is something that can't be avoided. We all need stuff, and stuff costs money. What you *can* do is lessen its impact on your wallet by modifying your shopping habits to make them as frugal as possible. While this subject has been touched on in a variety of other chapters so far (i.e., Chapter 6 and Chapter 9), this chapter looks at more general ways that you can fine-tune your shopping techniques to realize more savings through shopping strategies, coupons, etc.

Do You Really Need It?

It's pretty easy to convince yourself that you desperately need something when you run across it in a store, but you can quickly get back to frugal sanity by taking a moment to ask yourself the following:

- Do I really need this, or do I only want it? The ability to recognize the difference between a want and a need is a key one when it comes to shopping.
- Do I already own something that I can use instead of this? (See "The Rule of Three" tip in this chapter for more on this.)

- Does a friend or relative have one I can borrow? This is a great question to ask when it comes to items that you use infrequently (i.e., an obscure power tool, a carpet cleaning machine, etc.).
- Is this item something I can live without? Even if it passes the want/need test, is this particular item that you see still something that you can do without?

Do Your Research Before Buying

When buying large items, it really pays off to do your research before you shop? Consider makes, models, different manufacturers, what sort of options you want, size . . . everything down to the color you'd prefer. This way you'll get what you want at the price you're willing to pay, and you can easily brush off an aggressive salesperson's attempts to push you toward something you don't want (or can't afford).

Curb Impulse Buying with an Allowance

While it may sound rather adolescent, putting yourself on a weekly "allowance" can greatly help to curb the urge to impulse buy. At the very least, you'll put off any purchases that go over your allotted weekly amount until the next allowance day, a period of time in which you'll have an opportunity to consider whether you really need the item in the first place.

Examine Perspective Purchases for Defects

If you're looking for a particular item and there are several in stock, examine them all for minor flaws, such as a button missing, a slight blemish on a piece of furniture, etc. This is an excellent starting point to haggle a few dollars off the asking price.

Disarm Yourself

When you're heading to a store to buy an item you need, "disarm yourself" by leaving credit cards, ATM cards, and your checkbook at home. Bring only one check to cover the item you wish to buy (or better yet, bring just enough cash to cover it) to completely kill the urge to impulse buy.

Shop at the End of the Month or Quarter

The best time to shop for big-ticket items is at the end of the month or quarter when salespeople are trying to meet their quotas. This is the time when they will be most receptive to giving you a better price on a major item.

Buy Before You Run Dry

Don't wait until you run out of an item to buy it. Constantly keeping an eye open for clearance or sale items and purchasing them before you need them will save you greatly, opposed to buying something at regular price.

Shopping with a Plan

When shopping for clothes and other items, always go into a shop with a plan. This way you can target sales, specials, etc. One of the worst things you can do when shopping for anything (but particularly clothes) is to buy on impulse.

Buy in Bulk

Buy foodstuffs and other items in bulk whenever possible, but make sure the items are nonperishable. Buying in bulk can save you much money over time, but perishable items that spoil before you can use them will negate any saving.

The Rule-of-Three

One handy tool to use when trying to evaluate whether or not you should buy something is the Rule-of-Three. If a particular item can be used three different ways, you won't waste your money. For example, a sleeper sofa can be used as seating for family and friends, as a spare bed for company, or as a comfortable and convenient place to park yourself or a loved one when recovering from the flu or other ailment. It passes the Rule-of-Three test.

Shopping in Season

This has been mentioned briefly in a couple of previous chapters, but shopping for items in season — be it turkeys, air conditioners, or houses — can save you a significant amount of money. The following list is broken down by month and covers the items you should target in each month:

January
- Bedding
- Blankets
- Computers
- Holiday decorations & accessories
- Quilts
- Small appliances
- Towels

February
- Bedding
- Coats
- Floor coverings
- Furniture
- Housewares

March
- Air conditioners
- China
- Corned beef (until St. Patrick's Day)
- Dryers
- Frozen foods
- Glassware
- Houses
- Storm windows
- Washers

April
- Eggs
- Kitchen stoves
- Paint
- Wallpaper
- Women's/girl's dresses, etc. (post-Easter sales)

May
- Radios
- Televisions
- Towels & linens

June
- Bedding
- Floor coverings
- Furniture
- Pianos

July
- Craft supplies

- Dryers
- Fabric
- Hot dogs, hamburger (particularly around the 4th)
- Paper goods (also around the 4th)
- Washers

August
- Air conditioners
- Bathing suits
- Children's clothing
- Fresh vegetables (concentrate on locally-grown produce)
- Patio and lawn furniture
- Pens, paper, other school supplies
- Rugs
- Summer footwear and clothing
- Towels, linens

September
- China
- Garden tools and implements
- Glassware
- Housewares
- Pens, paper, and other school supplies
- Root vegetables such as carrots, potatoes, etc.

October
- Cars
- Fabrics
- Fishing gear
- Houses
- Rugs

November
- Autumn decorations
- Flour
- Ham
- Houses
- Quilts, blankets
- Space heaters
- Sugar
- Turkeys

December
- Flour
- Holiday decorations and accessories (after the 25th)
- Houses
- Sugar
- Turkeys

Double Up on Coupons

Unless otherwise stated, you can usually use both a manufacturer's and store coupon on one item, saving yourself double. Read the coupon's fine print to see if you can take advantage of this.

One handy tool to use when trying to evaluate whether or not you should buy something is the Rule-of-Three. If a particular item can be used three different ways, you won't waste your money. For example, a sleeper sofa can be used as seating for family and friends, as a spare bed for company, or as a comfortable and convenient place to park yourself or a loved one when recovering from the flu or other ailment. It passes the Rule-of-Three test.

Find a Coupon Exchange Group

Search in your area or online for a coupon exchange group. You probably run across many coupons for items that you don't use, and why let them go to waste? Coupon exchange programs let you barter for coupons that more closely meet your needs, and you have the added benefit of interacting with like-minded frugal individuals. From such relationships are friendships born.

Organize Your Coupons

Coupons are only good if you use them. Collect only those you use (or keep others to trade), and make sure they're organized so you don't lose track of them. Pick up a cheap organizer at a dollar store and place the coupons together by categories.

You Have... Mail-Order

Compare mail order prices with those you would pay in the store. Many times you can find stuff cheaper by mail-order, and you can't beat the convenience (you'll also be better able to resist impulse buying and you will save on gas).

Don't Fall for Malls

Avoid the lure of malls whenever possible, as there is just too much shopping temptation packed into one place. It's pretty easy to find yourself drifting out of control as you pass store after store. If you do need to visit a mall for a particular item, try to park as close as possible to the store you're visiting, so you can use its external entrance and avoid the internal gauntlet of walking through the whole mall to get to the store.

Target Alternative Shopping Venues

Many of the items that you need can be found by concentrating your shopping at so-called "alternative" stores. These include consignment stores, thrift stores, salvage shops, warehouse clubs, and yard sales (see Chapter 16 for a wealth of tips on how to get the most out of hosting or shopping at a yard sale).

Shop Online

The Internet offers a number of perks for shoppers, one of the best being the ability to easily "shop around" for the lowest price for almost anything, and from the comfort of your own home. Sites such as Epinions.com (http://www.epinions.com/) and StoreStory.com (http://www.storestory.com/) let you browse through other shoppers' opinions of numerous online stores, while shopping tools like MySimon.com (http://www.mysimon.com/) offer the ability to compare prices over a wide range of sites. Auction sites such as eBay (http://www.ebay.com/) can also be a treasure trove in terms of saving on a nearly endless assortment of new and used items.

Chain/Discount Stores

Try to shop as often as possible at chain or discount stores. It sounds obvious, but spending some time comparing prices for similar items at these and other stores can be a real eye-opener.

In Terms of Stores, Convenience Does Not Equal Frugal

Convenience stores sure are convenient, but they are also generally much more expensive than your average grocery store. It is not much convenience stores' fault. They just have to mark products higher to gain a profit. As a frugal shopper, you should avoid them unless absolutely necessary.

When In The Market for Furniture

One of the favorite advertising choices of furniture sellers is the newspaper. If you're in the market to purchase a couch or dining room furniture set, keep an eye open for such ads in your local newspaper.

Trendy Shopping

Avoid the trends! Trendy clothes will almost universally come with inflated prices, due to demand. As such, avoid them whenever possible.

Buy X, Get Y Free

Many times, stores will try to entice you into buying an expensive item by giving away another item with its purchase. While the lure of "free" is certainly strong, avoid this ploy, particularly if the free item is something you'd never purchase anyways.

Buy X, Get X Free II

Similarly, avoid the buy one, get one free scheme. If you're watching your prices carefully, you'll notice that stores will invari-

Convenience stores sure are convenient, but they are also generally much more expensive than your average grocery store. It is not the convenience stores' fault. They have to mark products higher to gain a profit. As a frugal shopper, you should avoid them unless absolutely necessary.

ably jack up the price of the item you're paying for immediately before the "special," meaning you don't really save. This can sometimes be a legitimate way to get two for the price of one, but you have to be careful to research the price carefully to make sure the store is not trying to con you.

Avoid Fancy Packaging

Without a doubt, fancy packaging can make a product very appealing, but don't give in to this "aesthetic trick," if you can avoid it. Expensive packaging will only add to the overall cost of the product, and you can often find the exact same thing, with plainer packaging, at a much lower price.

We'll Meet or Beat the Competitor's Price

Many stores have policies where they will meet or beat their competitors' prices on products. Searching these stores out can save you a considerable amount of money.

Be Mindful of Sales Taxes

Be mindful of the sales tax county-to-county or state-to-state. These can really add up, particularly on large items, but you should also be aware that you may be liable for sales taxes on big-ticket items (such as vehicles) in your own state or county. Of course, for items like stereos and refrigerators, local and state taxes are largely collected on the honor system.

Check All Sales Receipts

Make sure you carefully check your sales receipts before leaving the store, particularly if you have purchased items on sale. Computerized registers (and the people who run them) make more mistakes than you might think, particularly if something have been placed on-special for that week.

Ask for Rain Checks

Did you show up at a store, only to find that the sale item you wanted was sold out? Flag down a store employee and ask about the possibility of getting a rain check on the item.

Don't Be Afraid of Returns

Don't be intimidated by stores. If something you purchase doesn't measure up the way you think it should, return it.

Not on Sale? Have Patience

Try to avoid purchasing anything that is not on sale. Everything goes on sale eventually, and patience will be well-rewarded, particularly if you use this strategy for all your purchases.

In the Mood for Shopping

Don't shop when you are feeling down or depressed. It's much easier to justify impulse purchases as something that will pick you up or make you feel better, when in reality you may just end up feeling worse when you realize later how much you've spent on something you really don't need. Instead of shopping, try taking a walk, visiting the grandchildren, or reading a good book.

14
Utilities

E lectricity, hot water, the phone, heating and cooling. . . . We take them all for granted today, and while they do make life easier, they also come with price tags that can vary wildly from household to household. The area of utility costs is another one where a little bit of work can pay off with sizeable savings that will stretch over years.

The following tips cover a range of "utility" topics, including refrigerators and other appliances, hot water, heating and cooling, phones, and more. You can find related tips in a variety of other chapters in this book, especially Chapter 1: Around The House and Chapter 4: Clothing.

Position the Refrigerator for Efficiency/...

To get the most efficiency out of your refrigerator, location is the key. You should position your refrigerator out of direct sunlight and away from heat sources, such as heating ducts and stoves.

... And Give It Space

A refrigerator will run most efficiently when you place it a place where air can completely circulate around it. Leave at least three inches between the refrigerator and any counters or walls. Also, make sure that you don't use the top as sort of an open-air junk drawer, as this will also restrict air circulation.

Vacuum Refrigerator Coils Periodically

By the same token, sliding the refrigerator away from the wall and vacuuming the coils once a year will help to keep your refrigerator running more smoothly. This is particularly important if you have pets that love to shed.

Disable Automatic Refrigerator Devices

If your refrigerator came equipped with an automatic device, such as an ice maker or butter warmer, disconnect it. These may be convenient, but they also waste a lot of electricity.

Keep the Freezer Full

Freezers work most effectively when they are full. If you don't have food to fill them up, take soda or water bottles, fill them two-thirds full of water and allow them to freeze. You'll also gain the added bonus of a ready supply of ice packs for picnicking and camping.

Refrigerator Door Maintenance

Check your refrigerator door gasket periodically to see if it has become worn, ripped, or ill-fitting. If it has, replace it to greatly increase your refrigerator's efficiency.

Avoid "Frost Free"

"Frost free" may sound like a more attractive refrigerator than a plug-it-in-and-forget-it unit, but it will also cost you more in energy costs. Go with a traditional model and defrost it by hand every six months. You'll also keep a better handle on the food within it and waste less this way.

Cool Dishes Before Adding Them to the Refrigerator

Don't put warm dishes and foods directly into the refrigerator. Let them cool first, or else you'll cause the refrigerator to run needlessly.

Ventilation Fan Use/Misuse

Be careful when using kitchen and bathroom ventilation fans that you don't leave them running longer than you need to. In wintertime, these fans can quickly suck all the heat from of your house. In summer, they can do the same with your "cool," if you use air conditioning (and losing one's cool is never good).

Garbage Disposal Strategy

If you must own and run a garbage disposal (note: composting is a much better alternative), always use cold water when running it, instead of hot. Your hot water heater will thank you.

Freezers work most effectively when they are full. If you don't have food to fill them up, take soda or water bottles, fill them two-thirds full of water and allow them to freeze. You'll also gain the added bonus of a ready supply of ice packs for picnicking and camping.

Use Your Dishwasher More Efficiently

Dishwashers have reached the stage where they are actually more efficient water-users than washing dishes by hand. Their efficiency breaks down in their drying cycle, though. You should always

disable this and open the door to let the dishes air-dry.

Clean Your Dryer Lint Screen

Your dryer will run more efficiently if you clean the lint screen each time before you run a load. A full lint screen will reduce airflow, meaning the dryer has to work harder and longer to dry your clothes.

Schedule Consecutive Dryer Loads

If you must use a dryer, try to schedule it so that you use it for consecutive loads. This way you'll be taking advantage of the heat from the preceding load to start the next.

Repair Leaking Faucets

Don't let a leaking faucet send your hard-earned dollars down the drain. At one drip per second, a faucet can waste around 400 gallons of water a year. Not only will you be paying for the water, but if it is heated, you'll also be paying for the wasted electricity or oil used to heat it. Leaking faucets are easily fixed, most requiring just the replacement of a washer.

Save Water in the Bathroom

Save water while brushing your teeth or doing dishes by turning off the water between use's, and when the water is on, use it minimally (i.e., not wide open).

Use Low-Flow Shower Heads & Faucet Aerators

Want to save up to 50 percent of the water you use? Install low-flow shower heads and faucet aerators. Using these, typical family of four will save up to 14,000 gallons of hot water per year.

Shorten Showers to Save Hot Water Costs

Minimizing the amount of time you spend in the shower can save you considerably in hot water charges. Fully two-thirds of the amount of your hot water costs go toward showering, and even by trimming a few minutes off your showers, you can save hundreds of gallons of water (and the resulting cost) per month. To really maximize your savings, turn off the water while soaping up.

Lower Your Water Heater Temperature

Lowering the temperature of your water heater from 115 to 110 degrees will save you considerably over time.

Insulate Hot Water Heaters and Hot Water Pipes

Insulate both your water heater and hot water pipes to realize considerable savings year-round. In terms of the heater, make sure that you don't cover the top or bottom of the tank, nor get insulated material anywhere near the thermostat or burner compartment. For the pipes themselves, you can either go with specialized insulation sleeves for use with hot water pipes, or make up your own out of strips of thin insulation.

Wash Clothes in Cold Water

When possible, wash your clothes in cold water. This can save you a whopping 75 percent in energy usage.

Consider a Home Energy Audit

To quickly zero in on what areas you should concentrate on in your heating and cooling system to best save money, consider scheduling a home energy audit. Your gas or electric utility may have a program in place to do this for free or at a greatly reduced cost. If not, they should be able to point you to a professional who can do it for a reasonable amount. Home energy audits quickly pay for themselves in both energy savings and in showing you what areas you should concentrate to lower your bills.

Ventilate Heat from the Kitchen During the Summer

In the summer, keep your kitchen cool by using ventilation fans to carry the stove's heat outside. The electricity to run the fan will cost considerably less than the cost of the electricity to run your cooling system harder to compensate. Of course, the alternative is also true. In the winter, keep the ventilation fan off to help heat your house.

Turn Summertime Furnace Pilot Lights Off

Does your furnace have a pilot light? If you aren't using your furnace for anything in the summertime, why would you keep the pilot light on? This can save you a few dollars a month, **but make sure that you actually turn it off and not just blow it out, or you could be facing a very dangerous situation when your cellar starts filling with gas.**

Use Vegetation to Cut Down on Energy Bills

Planting vegetation around your house is one easy way to cut down on your energy bills, particularly if your area really heats up in the summer. Trees and bushes planted around your house will block a lot of the sunlight that would normally strike it.

Weatherize Windows for Big Savings

Make sure you weatherize your windows properly in the wintertime. This alone can save you a considerable amount of money, as well as make your house more enjoyable to live in. There are many different products you can use to achieve this, from simple plastic sheets to weather-stripping or putty. Run your hands around windows, doors, and outlets to feel for drafts (or use a candle and see where you get the most flicker), and then concentrate on getting the highest drafts under control first.

Dress Indoors for the Season

One of the biggest things you can do to assist in your heating/cooling bills is to dress for the season. Dress in several loose layers in the winter, and when you're cuddling up on the couch at night to read or watch TV, make sure you do so under a thick blanket. In the summer, go barefoot and wear loose-fitting light clothes such as t-shirts and shorts. Not only will you be more comfortable, your energy bills will be lower.

Check Ducts for Leaks

Leaking ductwork can contribute greatly to your heating costs. Consider having a professional check your ducts to see how efficient they are. Alternately, your local utility may have a program to do this for you for free or at a significantly reduced cost. If you have some form of maintenance program in place, where they come yearly to clean your furnace anyway, ask if they'll also check your ducts.

Use Airlocks to Cut Down on Energy Loss

In cold winter climates, one of the best ways you can cut down on energy/heat loss in your house is to employ an "airlock." Yes, think science fiction movies. Essentially, an airlock is an area that exists between two doors that you must go through to enter your house. This can either be an existing porch structure, or even a simple 2 x 4 and plastic structure that you add to your main door. The whole idea is that you go through one door before opening another, keeping the cold gusts from flowing into your house, and the hot air from flowing out.

Only Heat What You Have To

If you have rooms you don't use often in the winter, close them up and make sure you close the heating vents or radiators in these rooms. If a room is not being used, you'll save money by not heating it. Even if it is used infrequently, opening the door and turning the heat back on will make it comfortable in a few minutes. Only heat what you must.

Woodstove Plusses

Consider installing a woodstove to help with your winter heating. Wood is a renewable resource, and you can often find it for free if you really try (take down a tree on your property, offer to fell and tote away a dead tree on a neighbor's property, etc.). Wood is also a reliable heat source in case a winter storm takes out your power for an extended period of time, crippling your furnace.

If you have rooms you don't use in the winter, close them up and make sure you close the heating vents or radiators in these rooms. If a room is not being used, you'll save money by not heating it. Even if it is used infrequently, opening the door and turning the heat back on will make it comfortable in a few minutes. Only heat what you must.

Close Chimney Flues When Not in Use

When not using your fireplace, close the flue. As long the flue is open, it will continue to draw heat up it. If there is no fire, it will just be draining the heat from your house.

Extend the Life of Furnace Filters

The life of furnace filters can be extended by vacuuming them regularly. While this can add several months to their lifetime, you should eventually replace a filter when it starts to look ragged or dust falls out when you shake it after vacuuming.

Making the Most of Passive Solar Heat

You can make use of passive solar heat to take a real chunk out of your heating bills. If you have southern-facing windows, keep them well-cleaned and open up the shades and curtains when the sun is shining. . . . It will also help if you have something large and dark in color (such as a brick wall or concrete floor) that will soak up the heat during the day and radiate it back out at night. When the sun goes down, make sure you close the curtains to retain the heat.

Kicking Passive Solar Up a Notch

You don't have a brick wall or concrete floor to soak up all that nice sunshine? You could try making your own simple solar heater. Get one or more five-gallon buckets (check with local restaurants. . . . they're usually tripping over them) and paint them black. Fill the buckets with water and set them in the sun. These could either be used as little solar heaters (they'll absorb heat during the day and radiate it back out at night), or you could use the hot water for some other purpose. Either way, it's free.

Before Calling, Know What You Want to Talk About

Keep long distance phone calls shorter by making a list of "talking points" that you want to cover. This is great for non-personal calls, but it can also be employed to a certain extent with personal calls as well.

Keep a Timer by the Phone

When you get on the phone for a long-distance call, particularly during peak hours, set a timer. This will help to keep your calls shorter and cut down on your costs.

Peruse Your Phone Plan for Waste

Pay close attention to your phone bill, and call the phone company to discuss other plans that might save you more money. For example, if you are paying a set amount for a predetermined number of calls, but you aren't making your minimum, you're probably spending more money than you need to. Gather up about three months worth of bills and get a feel for how you use your phone; then give the phone company a jingle to see how you can save.

Eliminate Unnecessary Phone Services

All the little perks you get on your phone, whether it's call waiting, party lines, caller ID, or other services, all cost extra money. If you don't use them, don't add to your phone bill by using them.

Optimize Your Cell Phone Plan

If you have a cell phone, keep track of the number of minutes you use per month and see if your plan can be trimmed. Look back through the past six months of bills. If you are falling well short of your allotted minutes per month, you're paying too much plan. Call your provider to get into a lower plan and save money.

Directory Assistance Alternatives

Directory assistance will also cost you a pretty penny. If you don't have a phone book for the area you are calling, consider using one of the Internet phone directories, such as one of the following:

Yellowbook.com (http://www.yellowbook.com/),
Switchboard.com (http://www.switchboard.com/), or
WhoWhere.com (http://www.whowhere.com/).

Don't *69

Resist the temptation to use *69 or *66 with your phone. These might be convenient, but they will also cost you extra each time you use them (this will vary, but both run around fifty cents a shot in many states).

Remove Long Distance from Your Second Phone Line

Do you have two phone numbers, one of which is used just for a computer? If so, that line is only used for local dial-up access, and you may be able to save money by removing the long distance access from it. This is usually a charge that is added to a line just to enable long distance (usually around $5), and if you don't need it, there is no reason to pay for it.

Phone Card Shopping Pointers

Planning on making a number of calls while on vacation or away from home for some other reason? Look into several different prepaid phone cards or calling cards to find one that fits your needs. These vary widely in terms of the cost per minute and additional surcharges.

The Cheapest Background Noise

If you're like me, you can't stand a completely quiet house and need some form of background noise. And, when it comes to background noise, your television could be unnecessarily costing you a mint. Go with a radio, as it uses much less power.

Cut Out or Cut Back On Premium Movie Stations

If you get cable or satellite TV, take a look at your bill and decide if the cost of the movie channels are really worth it. At the very least, think about cutting back to the bare minimum during the late spring to early fall months, when you should be outside enjoying other pursuits anyhow. If you really can't live without these options full time, turn these channels back on in the winter to catch up on what you missed in the summer. You could also alternate them: one block of movie channels one month, one block the next, etc. This way you get all the movies you want and you only have to pay for one block per month.

Pay Attention to Energy Guide Labels on Appliances

When the time comes to replace old appliances with new (as painful as it is), make certain that you shop around to find the most energy efficient ones you can (especially true of things like air conditioners, furnaces, etc.). In addition to comparing prices, look for the "Energy Guide Labels" on products and compare them for future energy costs. Focusing on buying the most efficient appliances will save you potentially hundreds of dollars a year in electric costs.

Electric Blanket Do's (More Like Don'ts)

Avoid the use of electric blankets and settle instead for more blankets on the bed (or sleep in socks and thick pajamas or a sweat suit). You create more than enough heat yourself, so you don't need an additional source. If you are completely addicted to an electric blanket to the point where this tip is nonsensical, make sure you don't leave the blanket turned on during the day.

Keep Waterbeds Well Insulated

A waterbed can really suck up the electricity (some sources claim that a waterbed heater can use more electricity than a water heater and refrigerator combined). If you really must have one, keep it well insulated during the day, using heavy comforters on the top and sides.

Shut Off those Lights!

You can save a considerable amount of money by simply shutting off lights when you leave a room. If you find yourself forgetting, consider installing some form of sensor that will do the job for you.

Use Timers to Save $ When on Vacation

When traveling, don't just leave a light on. The use of timers will not only give you peace of mind, it will also save you money. Set the timer to turn the lights on only during night hours, or work with a couple of timers to turn on different lights in the house to confuse would-be burglars into thinking someone is home.

Participate in Off-Hour Rate Programs

Does your utility offer off-hour rates or load management programs? Give the utility a call to see if it does, and determine how you can participate. These programs can save you a considerable amount of money in the course of a year if you sign up for them and know how to get the most out of them.

Eliminate "Ghost Loads"

Think your appliances are not sucking any power when they are turned off? Not necessarily so. Many appliances, such as televisions and microwaves, have built into them what are known as "ghost load." built into them. Ghost loads are small parts of the appliances that constantly use a little electricity, even when the appliance is shut off. One way to totally kill ghost loads is to unplug appliances when they are not being used. A great way to handle this is to use an extension cord that allows you to shut off all appliances with a simple switch.

Meter Fun

Learn to read your meter and turn your electric usage into a game. Everyday, at the same time, go outside and jot down the meter reading (your utility company can give you information on how to do this). For the first couple of weeks or so, note the numbers and how much power you use day to day. When you get comfortable with reading the meter, start tinkering with the utilities in your house to see what appliances uses the most power and set goals to try to get the meter numbers (and your bill) lower.

Go to the Source to Ask about Savings

When in doubt, reach out. Take every bill you pay each month and get in touch with the companies, utilities, etc. from to determine if there is anything you can do to reduce your monthly costs. It never hurts to ask, and you'll find that many of these sources are very helpful in suggesting ways to save, recommending different pricing plans, etc.

15
Yard Sales

Yard sales, barn sales, garage sales, church bazaars . . . call them what you want; they are the best way to either get rid of your junk and make a little money, or add to your junk for just a little money. The following tips will get you started in running your own sale, or help you make the most out of visiting someone else's sale.

Running A Yard Sale

Make Sure Your Sale Is Legal

Communities are all over the map when it comes to regulating such things as yard sales. Remember to check with your town or city to make sure such things are allowed, and check whether you need a permit to hold one.

The More the Merrier

"Sharing" your yard sale with neighbors or friends makes sense on a number of levels. For one, you can split up the work involved, making a sale much easier on you. More people involved equals more items, which in turn will draw a larger crowd. You'll also get to split the cost of any newspaper ads you place to advertise your sale.

Advertising Your Sale

There are many ways to advertise a yard sale to insure a steady stream of traffic. If you live on a major road, often posting just a couple of large signs in front of your house will do the trick. Your local paper's classifieds section is a great way to reach potential buyers for just a few bucks (browse through other yard sale listings to get a feel for what your ad should say). Other possibilities include posting signs on grocery store or community bulletin boards or attaching them on telephone poles in your neighborhood (check with the board owners or local authorities to make sure such things are permissible).

Selecting the Right Date

The date you choose to run your sale can make all the difference. Saturdays are the most popular days to host a yard sale, followed by Sundays (many people run their sales over both days). Avoid holidays and special "event" days. If people are relaxing at a July 4th parade or BBQ, they won't be at your sale.

Run an Electrical Test Cord

If you're selling appliances or other electrical equipment, make sure that you have an extension cord handy so the perspective buyers can try these items out. It's probably also a good idea to keep the cord out of the way until it is needed, so that it doesn't create a traffic hazard as people browse through your sale.

Display Large Items Prominently

Place large items, such as cribs, TVs, and furniture, in the front area of your sale to draw in interested buyers who happen to be driving by. This will also help to attract people to the rest of your sale, where the less prominent items are located.

Frisk Your Clothes Before Putting Them on the Sale Table

Take care to go through any clothing you plan to sell, particularly coats. At the very least, you could also be selling personal items buried in the pockets. At the most, coat pockets could contain money, bank statements, or other receipts with personal/financial information containing.

Ambience

Having relaxing or easy-listening music playing in the background at your sale will not only create a pleasant browsing atmosphere, but it will also allow buyers to discuss items amongst themselves without feeling that they have to whisper.

Set Up on the Street

Set up your check-out table on the street that is. Setting yourself up right at the edge of your sale will offer two distinct plusses: You can keep an eye open for any buyers who "forget" to pay and you can be available to answer questions from anyone driving by on the street.

Cleanliness is Next to . . . Soldliness

Make sure you clean up any items that you are putting up for sale. Not only will it make a better overall impression on visitors to your yard sale, but clean items will sell much more quickly than those with a layer of dust or several years of grime on them.

Yard Sale Pricing

When pricing items for a yard sale, avoid the usual retail ploy of pricing items at $2.99, $5.98, etc. You'll find it much easier to make change (and a lot less of a hassle) to price items either at rounded out dollar amounts, or twenty-five, fifty, and seventy-five cents for smaller items.

Don't Forget a Calculator

Unless you're a math whiz or have a strong desire to bone up on your arithmetic skills with a pen and paper, keeping a calculator on hand will greatly simplify the process of "ringing people out."

Paper or Plastic?

Don't forget to lay in a stockpile of paper or plastic bags so that visitors to your sale can easily carry away their purchases. It's also good to have a pile of old newspapers on hand to wrap up and safeguard any breakables you're selling.

Group Similar Items

Grouping similar items together — for example, kitchen items on one table, books on another — will not only make your sale easier to navigate for those visiting it, but will also lead to increased sales.

Sell Beverages

If the day of your sale is a hot one, you can increase your profits by selling sodas. Buy the sodas cheaply (in bulk and on sale, if possible), ice them down in a cooler, and you're set to go. Consider only offering brands or flavors that you'll drink yourself so that any leftovers won't go to waste. Also, think about putting a trash can near the entrance of your sale so that your lawn doesn't get littered with empty cans and other trash.

Caveat Emptor

Buyer beware! To avoid any problems the day after your yard sale, make sure that you prominently post a sign at your checkout table letting everyone know "All Sales Are Final." While the chances of anyone looking for their money back on an item are slim, this should kill any possibility of that happening.

Cash Only, Please

While you can certainly accept checks if you're feeling brave, it's really not a great idea. Looking at a check, you can never tell if the account it's drawn from is valid or not. Add to this the fact that your bank may stick you with a hefty returned-check fee, and cash-only is really the best way to go.

Don't Give in to Haggling too Soon

Haggling is a yard-sale staple for some, but don't give in too early in the sale. If someone tries to talk you down in price early on, politely decline. Additionally, you can either tell the buyer that you might come down in price later in the day, or offer to take his or her name and phone number in case the item doesn't sell.

Visiting Someone Else's Sale

Plan Your Route

One of the best places to start planning a day of hitting yard sales is your local paper's classifieds section. Browse through the listings, making notes on locations and any particular items mentioned that you might especially be interested in. Once you have your list, get a local map and plan out the order to hit the sales. Planning out your route will keep you from running back and forth all over town, saving you gas and time.

Bare in Mind a Sale's Location

Where a sale is located can often give hints as to what sort of items you'll find there . . . and what sort you won't. For example, a yard sale in a retirement community is probably not the best place to find clothing for children, but antiques are another matter entirely. Sales held in "nicer" neighborhoods will also tend to have higher quality items for sale.

When to Hit Sales

Arriving early at yard sales is obviously a good strategy in that you'll find a better selection of items, not to mention the bargain "treasures" that many professional yard salers seek out. Don't rule out visiting sales later in the day, though. As those hosting sales look to get rid of as much as possible towards the end of the day, this is often where you'll find the best bargains or the best atmosphere for haggling.

Yard Sale Currency

If you can, stock your wallet or purse with "yard sale currency": smaller bills and change. It's easier for all involved if you buy something priced at twenty five cents with a quarter as opposed to a $20 bill.

Target Church Sales for Low Prices

Generally speaking, you'll tend to find better prices at church or other types of fund-raising sales. Since all the items at such sales have been donated, however, you may find the overall quality not to be as good as at "private" sales.

Fanny-Pack Trumps Purse

When you are frequenting yard sales, you'll want to keep your hands as free as possible so that you can really check out items. Either keep your cash in your pockets, or consider wearing a fanny pack.

Carefully Examine "As Is" Items

As most items at yard sales are sold "as is," it is important to carefully examine them to make sure they have all the right parts, are not damaged in any significant way, etc. This is particularly true of electrical/electronic devices. The yard sale operator should have some way to plug in such items so that you can test them.

Avoid Unsafe or Recalled Items

Try to avoid purchasing unsafe or recalled items at yard sales. Unsafe items can include old appliances with frayed cords or hair dryers that do not have the large, rectangular safety plugs that are now standard. Recalled items can be a little trickier to spot, but many times these will be found in the form of children's items, such as cribs or car seats. If you have a question about a particular item, you can call the Consumer Product Safety Commission at 1-800-638-2772, or visit them online at http://www.cpsc.gov/.

Mine!

If you find an item but are unsure about buying it, carry it around with you while you browse through the other items for sale. If you decide you don't want it, you can always put it back. If you decide later on you do want it, it's already in your hand and not someone else's.

Let the Seller Name a Price

It will almost always be to your benefit to let the seller name the price for a certain item. If you feel the price is too high, you can always try to haggle him or her down. Too low? You've just found yourself a real bargain!

Put Your Best Haggle-Face Forward

If you thrive on haggling at yard sales, make sure you put your best "face" forward to assure that the seller will be more receptive to your counter offers. Leave the pearls, diamonds, and designer clothes at home. Similarly, leave the Rolls Royce in the garage and take the beat-up pickup truck instead.

If Haggling Fails

If the seller refuses to come down on the price of an item that you consider to be too high, offer to leave your name and number. If the item hasn't sold by the end of the day, the seller may be much more willing to consider your lower price.

You're Under No Obligation To Buy

Don't feel that simply because you're at a sale you have to be "nice" and buy at least something. If you don't see anything you either really want or need, thank the person running sale, wish them luck, and move on to the next sale.

16
Travel

When considered a bit of a luxury, many find that traveling is something that pays for itself through relaxation, discovery, and just generally, educating oneself to the wonderful places and cultures out there in the world. The following tips cover all aspects of frugal traveling, from planning for trips and getting to destinations as cheaply as possible, to strategies for saving money on hotels, restaurants, rental cars, and cruises.

Tap Friends/Family for Travel Advice

One good way to get advice on a particular location is to seek out family or friends that have traveled there before. This can provide a valuable source of information on hotels, restaurants, and attractions/sights, but remember to take it all with a grain of salt and back it up with your own research. What appeals to one person may appall another.

Don't Try to Do Everything while on Vacation

Don't feel that you have to run all the time and bust your budget seeing everything when you travel to a particular location. Saving some sights for next time will give you a reason to return, and your vacation will be more frugal and relaxing.

Plan Ahead when It Comes to Sight-seeing

Definitely do some planning before you even arrive at your destination. Sit down with a map of the area and decide what you want to visit or see, and then block out your time day by day. This will not only give some structure to your vacation in terms of doing everything you want, but it will also save you money when it comes to transportation charges (i.e., you can plan to see attractions grouped in specific areas on specific days).

Target Off-Season for Savings

Travel off-season to really save money and cut down on the crowds. If you're not looking forward to the thought of Florida in the summer or Norway in the winter, consider scheduling your travel for the edge of the peak season, either just before or just after. Be sure to contact hotels to find out when their rates switch to off-peak.

Consider a Package Deal

Selecting a package deal that includes airfare, hotel, transfers, and some meals or other extras can save you considerably over trying to cover them yourself piecemeal. Definitely keep your eyes open for these sorts of deals, but scrutinize them carefully to make sure that you will enjoy all elements of the package.

Look into Tours to Save

Instead of traveling individually, consider booking an escorted tour to save around 20 percent or more above what you would pay by yourself.

When Travel, Not Destination, Is Your Goal

Just looking to get away and not too particular where you wind up? Or, perhaps you have a few options on your list? Let the cost of airfare be your deciding factor. Flights to any area can fluctuate wildly, due to a number of factors. If travel, not destination, is your main goal, select the cheapest destination and start planning to have fun once you get there!

Pack Light

Minimizing how much you cram into your suitcase(s) will not only make it easier to travel, but it can also save you in terms of excess baggage charges. You'll also have more room to lug back souvenirs.

Chaperone Your Way to a Cheap Trip

If you don't mind playing the role of chaperone, you can often travel for free (or at a greatly reduced price) by volunteering to accompany educational or scientific trips.

Travel with a Group

Traveling with a group of several people is not only more fun than doing it alone, but you can also save a considerable amount of money traveling this way.

Check for Group Discounts

Don't forget to ask for discounts wherever you go, particularly if you are part of a large, recognized group. While hotels and other establishments may not publicly list that they offer discounts, many do offer discounts for groups such as AAA, AARP, and the like, and these can save you considerably if you are a card-carrying member.

Ask About Specials

Don't be afraid to ask about specials wherever you go. Many times the hotel, activity, etc. where you find yourself will offer specials or discounts, but they will not go out of their way to advertise them.

When Traveling, Avoid the ATM

Traveler's checks offer a number of perks over other methods of payment. One way is to help you cut down on both the inconvenience of trying to find ATMs and the cost you'll incur in multiple transaction fees.

Shop the Internet for Cheap Flights

The Internet can be one of your best tools when it comes to shopping for the best air fares. Sites like the ones listed below are quick and easy to use. For the best bargains, try hitting several to do a little comparison shopping:

http://www.bestfares.com
http://www.cheapairlines.com
http://www.economytravel.com
http://www.expedia.com
http://www.flycheap.com
http://www.orbitz.com
http://www.priceline.com
http://www.smarterliving.com
http://www.travelocity.com

Overbooking: Doing the Airline a Favor for Free Flights

Are you fairly flexible when it comes to when you get to a destination? Consider opening yourself up to helping an airline when it overbooks. Occasionally, an airline will overbook its flights and ask for volunteers to give up their seat. This is an easy way to get free flights, particularly if you don't have to be somewhere at a specific time. If you decide to go this route, try to schedule your flight for Monday morning or Friday afternoon, the times when most overbookings occur.

Your Savings: Not a Casualty of Price Wars

They are called price wars. When one airline announces that it is slashing prices to a particular destination, you can be reasonably assured that other airlines will be doing the same in a short period of time. If you hear of one airline offering deep discounts to a particular spot, look around to see what its competitors are offering before blindly jumping on it.

Keep Your Travel Dates Flexible

Flexibility in what dates and times you are willing to travel can often save you a sizable amount of money. The more you're willing to bend to meet airline needs (and fill seats on flights they have trouble filling), the more you will save.

Fly Off-Peak

Get better deals on airline flights by flying at off-peak times.

Shun First Class

It sounds like a given, but it should be repeated anyways: Fly economy class instead of first class to save a lot of money. It may not be as comfortable, but grin and bare it. Work through your discomfort by concentrating on the thought of using the money you saved to better enjoy your destination.

Gain Free Air Miles with Your Credit Card

Your credit card can be a valuable source of free air miles. Check with your credit card company to see if its gives free miles for every purchase you make. If so, use your card for as many purchases as you can, making sure that you pay off your balance every month so that interest rates don't nullify your free miles benefit.

Flying Into Close-Enough Airports to Save Money

Shopping around for a cheap flight is frequently the best way to save money while flying, but sometimes it's just impossible to find a deal. One way around this is to fly into a nearby airport and then take a connecting flight, bus, or train to your destination. Some examples of this strategy include:

- Washington, D.C.: Consider flying into Baltimore instead of Washington, D.C. Not only will this tend to be less expensive, but in this new era of terrorism, also less intrusive.
- New York City: Check out the price of flights to Newark.
- Los Angeles: There are many local airports around Los Angeles that may be less expensive to fly into, including Burbank, Orange County, and Ontario (California).
- London: Look into the pricing and availability of flights flying into Birmingham.

When to Stay In-City, When to Stay In-Country

You often can save on hotel costs by staying in the city on weekends and then moving out into the surrounding country areas during the week.

Consider a Hostel

While not for every traveler, hostelling can be an excellent and inexpensive way to travel through much of the world. One of the best websites for finding over 6,000 hostels worldwide is hostels.com (http://www.hostels.com/). As an example, a recent search for a hostel in London, one month out, returned prices as low as $16 a night.

Avoid Hotel Laundries

If you use the hotel laundry to launder your clothes, you might as well stuff your pockets with cash before sending it out. You can save a lot of money by scouting out a local laundromat or dry cleaner.

Choose Your Cell Phone over Your Hotel Phone

Your cell phone is a much better, and cheaper, option for long-distance calls than your hotel room phone.

Mini-Bar Avoidance

Those mini-bars might be mega-convenient, but they can also be mega-expensive. Save your travel cash stash by shopping for snacks and beverages at the local convenience store (or, better yet, search out a local grocery store).

 Shopping around for a cheap flight is frequently the best way to save money while flying, but sometimes it's just impossible to find a deal. One way around this is to fly into a nearby airport and then take a connecting flight, bus, or train to your destination.

Don't Rent Cars at the Airport

If you need to rent a car, try to avoid doing so at the airport. Prices will tend to be more expensive than at other agencies located a bit more "out," and you may face additional surcharges. It may be convenient the airport, but convenience almost always comes at a price.

Check for Membership Discounts

Much like when renting a room or visiting a local attraction, always check for membership rate discounts when renting a vehicle. AAA, AARP, and similar groups you might belong to could save you significantly on rental charges.

Rent for Utility, Not Looks

Renting cars from late-model car agencies or insurance car rental agencies may not provide you with the classiest ride in town, but such vehicles will get you where you're going at a fraction of the cost of other car rental agencies.

Keep an Eye on Gas Prices when Renting Cars

When renting a car, keep an eye open for competing gas prices wherever you are. Prices can vary considerably, and usually you can find lower prices within the city limits than in outlying areas.

Get in the Driver's Seat with Taxis

If you need to rent a car, try to avoid doing so at the airport. Prices will tend to be more expensive than at other agencies located a bit more "out," and you may face additional surcharges. It may be convenient, but convenience at the airport almost always comes at a price.

Don't get taken to the cleaners by the local taxi drivers (unless that was your destination anyhow). Ask at your hotel about costs for cab rides to various places. In some instances, you can even haggle over price with the driver before ever getting into the taxi.

Choose the Bus over the Taxi

Seek out and use the local bus or subway routes to save what you would pay if you used taxis to get around. You'll also get a lot more of the atmosphere of the city this way.

Alternatives to Restaurants

One area that will quickly add up when vacationing is food. Restaurants can be fantastic experiences, but you should view them as special treats, and not de facto food sources when vacationing. A much better and cheaper option is to seek out local grocery stores and supermarkets. Many now offer soup or salad bars, as well as other culinary conveniences, and the simple truth is that you could feed yourself for a whole week at most supermarkets for the cost of one or two meals out. By all means, hit a restaurant, or three, as a special treat, but don't rely on them for all your meals or your wallet will be much the lighter.

Dine with the Locals

When seeking a unique dining experience, consider checking out some local restaurants instead of those geared towards tourists. You'll generally pay a lot less and get a much better "feel" for the flavor of an area. In order to find the best of these establishments, ask people who work at the hotel or area shops.

Pack Your Own Snacks

Save money and time, keep up your energy, and improve your nutritional intake by packing your own snacks before heading out. You can do this initially or by selectively stocking up at cheaper grocery stores (as opposed to convenience stores) along the way.

Cruises: The Best Deal for Your Dollars?

To obtain the best value for the travel dollar, consider cruise ships. There are now so many plying the seas, heading to virtually every destination (OK, not Idaho), that you can find real deals at rates that are comparable to a decade ago.

Singles Saving Money on Cruises

Single travelers on cruises can save money by offering to have a roommate assigned to them. Considering how small most cruise ship rooms are, though, this is not without its risks.

Be Careful of Cruise Ship "Extras"

Cruise ships are amazing in the extras they now offer, but think carefully before taking advantage of everything. While many things will be free, many others will cost you dearly. Make sure you are aware of all charges for a particular activity beforehand, and carefully consider whether it is something you really want to shell out the cash for.

17
Specifically For Seniors

While this book is mainly comprised of general tips in a variety of categories that anyone can use to save money, there are some tips that are specifically geared towards seniors. We've collected these tips in this chapter and organized them under a number of topics, including discounts, travel, financial planning, health, and online resources.

Discounts

Ask for Senior Discounts

Stores, restaurants, movie theaters, contractors, parks, and other recreation areas, services. . . . You'd be surprised at the number of businesses out there that offer some form of senior discount, and many of them have one thing in common: You have to ask to receive them. While many businesses offer them, few will actually advertise the fact. Don't be afraid to ask anyone you do business with if such discounts are available.

Join AARP

Formerly known as the American Association of Retired Persons, the AARP is made up of over 35 million seniors, a sizable block that allows the organization to leverage discounts for its members on everything from travel (i.e., hotels, car rentals, airlines) to insurance (i.e., health, auto, home-owners). Savings can run you up to 50 percent if you're a member (although you should still shop around to make sure you're getting the cheapest rate available). AARP also offers a number of other perks for members, such as services, publications, and advice for living well. Membership is available to those fifty and over for $12.50 a year (this includes membership for both you and your spouse/partner).

AARP
601 E. Street NW Washington, DC 20049
Phone: 1-888-OUR-AARP
Website: http://www.aarp.org/

Marriott's Senior Discount Program

Many hotel chains offer their own discount programs to entice seniors to stay with them. One of these is Marriott, which *used* to offer a 10 percent AARP discount before dropping it in favor of a 15 percent discount for any senior sixty two and over. To participate, either mention the program when you call to make a reservation, or check the "Marriott Senior Discount (age sixty two and above)" box if making a reservation through the Marriott website.

Marriott
Phone: 1-888-236-2427
Website: http://www.marriott.com

Airline Discounts

There are many ways to get discounts on airline tickets, including through the AARP or through price-comparison websites such as

Expedia.com (http://www.expedia.com) or Travelocity.com (http://www.travelocity.com). Some airlines also offer senior discount programs or clubs that you can join to realize significant savings on flight ticket, and other travel-related things such as hotels and car rentals. One such airline is United, which offers its Silver Wings Plus club. After joining, seniors can find deals on vacation combinations, cruises, and domestic or international flights. At the time of writing this, membership cost $75 for two years (you'll also get $1,000 in travel saving discounts and offers) or $225 for a lifetime membership (which includes $2,500 in discounts and offers).

Silver Wings Plus
21744 Network Place
Chicago, Illinois 60673
Phone: 1-800-720-1765
Website: https://www.silverwingsplus.com/

Amtrak Senior Citizen Discounts

If you'd rather travel by rail than air, Amtrak can help those over sixty two with a 15 percent discount off most fares. Amtrak does have a number of restrictions (i.e., the discount doesn't apply to sleeper accommodations or the Auto Train), but Amtrak offer's a number of other discounts as well, such as 10 percent discount on North American Rail Passes.

Amtrak
Phone: 1-800-USA-RAIL (1-800-872-7245)
Website: http://www.amtrak.com/ (do a search for "seniors")

SeniorDiscounts.com

Those with access to the Internet will find a great resource in

SeniorDiscounts.com. This database allows you to search for local discounts in a wide range of categories, from ski areas to retailers. To use this free service, enter your city/state or zip code and select the categories where you wish to find discounts. SeniorDiscounts.com will then post all discounts stored in its database that meet your specifications, outlining exactly what the discount pertains to, the cost, and the age requirements to claim it. It also offer's a free newsletter and weekly prizes through something they call the Senior Internet Challenge.

SeniorDiscounts.com
PO Box 541912
Houston, TX 77254-1912
Phone: 1-877-924-2023
Fax: 1-713-522-5114
Website: http://www.seniordiscounts.com/
E-mail: Pete@seniordiscounts.com

Travel

Elderhostel

While travel is covered prominently in the Discounts section of this chapter, there are a couple more travel resources for seniors that need to be mentioned (be sure to also check out Chapter 17). The first of these is Elderhostel, an organization that has been offering educational and travel opportunities for seniors since 1975. Two hundred thousand older adults participate every year in the ten thousand programs Elderhotel provides in more than 90 countries. Many of its programs are set up as educational "themed" trips, complete with lectures, field trips, and cultural excursions. For example, in one program you can trace the footsteps of Lewis and Clark. In another, you get to visit all the French villages where Monet lived, and then view his masterpieces in a number of Parisian museums.

There are no membership fees of any kind to participate in an Elderhostel program. All you have to do is sign up for a program itself. While you have to pay your own way to get to the starting point of a program, once you're there, a very decent daily fee (for US/Canadian trips, usually $115 per day) covers all your meals, accommodations, tours, etc. The best way to get started with Elderhostel is to request a catalog of its programs, which comes in three different flavors: US & Canadian, International, and Adventures Afloat.

Elderhostel
11 Avenue de Lafayette
Boston, MA 02111-1746
Phone: 1-877-426-8056
Website: http://www.elderhostel.org/

Seniors Home Exchange

Another unique resource for those with access to the Internet is the Seniors Home Exchange. This is essentially a giant database that those over fifty can use to "swap" their house with someone else from another part of the country or world. The Senior Home Exchange currently has over 1,603 "exchanges" listed from 38 countries, and you can easily browse through them by location, or do a keyword search. This option is particularly convenient for finding people who are interested in swapping houses with someone else in a particular area. This resource is a great way to cut your accommodation expenses while traveling down to zero!

Seniors Home Exchange
Web site: http://www.seniorshomeexchange.com/

Financial Planning

When to Retire

When is the best time to retire and start collecting social security? Every situation is different, but understanding how the system works and knowing the pros and cons of taking early, as opposed to full retirement, can help you make the right decision for your unique situation.

The amount you make each month through social security will depend to a large extent on when you begin collecting benefits. While you can start taking benefits at age 62, you'll make more per month if you wait until full retirement. This is dependent on when you were born. For example, for those born in 1937 or earlier, full retirement age is 65. Those born later will have a few more months added to their full retirement age, such as those born in 1942, who are looking at 65 years and 10 months to retire with full benefits. If you retire between 62 and your full retirement age, you'll see a reduction in your monthly payments, the theory being that you'll receive the same amount of money throughout the rest of your life, just spread out over more years at a lower monthly payment.

So which is better, early or full retirement? This will actually depend on a number of factors, including your financial state. Experts say that you might be better off taking early retirement if your health is poor or you have a family history of low life expectancy. Taking early retirement in these situations means that you'd stand a better chance to receive more benefits over the course of your life than if you waited to retire (and obviously, the reverse is also true: if you are in good health with a family history of high longevity, you might be better off waiting to take full retirement). Contact the Social Security Administration or a financial planner to get advise on this tailored to your unique needs.

> Social Security Administration
> Office of Public Inquiries
> Windsor Park Building
> 6401 Security Blvd.
> Baltimore, MD 21235
> Phone: 1-800-772-1213
> Website: http://www.ssa.gov/

Social Security and Continuing to Work

You can actually continue to work and still draw social security, but you should be aware that there is a limit at which your social security benefit will be reduced. At the moment, the limit is $11,640 (it gets adjusted occasionally for inflation). In other words, for every $2 you make over the limit, your social security benefits will be reduced by $1. Note that this limit does not include such income streams as pensions, annuities, investment income, interest, or veteran/government/military benefits. Careful planning is the key to maximizing your income while still keeping your social security benefits intact.

Solving Pension Problems

Is your past employer not paying you your pension money, or paying only part of it? You can get help with this problem from the federal government, specifically the U.S. Department of Labor, Employee Benefits Security Administration. Call or write this department for information on your local contact point, and also to inquire about the wide variety of pension publications it put's out.

U.S. Department of Labor

EBSA

Division of Technical Assistance and Inquiries

Room N-5619

200 Constitution Avenue N. W.

Washington, D.C. 20210

Phone: 1-866-275-7922

Website: http://www.pbgc.gov/

Get Help in Preparing Your Taxes

It is appropriate, given that they are to blame for it in the first place, the federal government (with the help of the AARP) is available there to help seniors unravel the mysteries of the tax code with free help. The Tax Counseling for the Elderly (TCE) program provides help in preparing federal and state income tax forms to low-income people, sixty and over, at a variety of community sites throughout the country. The AARP runs the part of the TCE known as Tax-Aide, at 9,000 sites throughout the country. Contact either to find the site nearest you.

Tax Aide

Phone: 1-888-227-7669

Website: http://www.aarp.org/money/taxaide

E-mail: taxaide@aarp.org

TCE

Phone: 1-800-829-1040

Give Gifts to Reduce Your Taxable Estate

To pay less estate tax on your assets when you die (and thus leave more to your children or beneficiaries), you can start dispensing money early as gifts. There is a limit to how much you can give per person per year, which is adjusted for inflation (in 2004, the amount was $11,000), so you should check to determine the current maximum. This rate is also based upon per person giving it. For example, both you and your spouse could give $11,000 per child or beneficiary in 2004, for a $22,000 total. You'll also need to establish a paper trail concerning these gifts, such as documentation regarding the transfer, copies of appraisals, and tax forms such as Form 709 (tax information regarding gifts can be found in Publication 950). Call the IRS at 1-800-829-1041 for more information or to receive publications and forms.

Reverse Mortgages

Seniors who find their nest egg dwindling may have a couple of sources of ready cash available in their homes and life insurance policies. In terms of the former, one way to convert home equity into cash is through a reverse mortgage. With a reverse mortgage, you essentially "sell" your house to a lender for a certain amount of money. This money is paid to you as a one-lump sum, through monetary payments, or is set up as a ready line of credit should you need it. So long as you continue to live in the house, the money doesn't have to be paid back, the theory being that upon your death, the house will be sold and the lender will get back the amount of money he's paid out, plus a small percentage to cover the cost of the loan.

There are a couple of downsides to reverse mortgages, the most obvious being that the lender, and not your children, will get the house. The lender will also keep track of what you are doing with the house, making sure that you continue to live there and pay the taxes and insurance. Still, this is a very viable option for those sixty two or older who find themselves strapped for cash and who have fully paid off their mortgages.

To obtain more information, contact the National Reverse Mortgage Lenders Association. This nonprofit organization offers a number of consumer guides and other valuable information on reverse mortgages (and they really know their business . . . their members are responsible for 90 percent of the reverse mortgages underwritten each year in the United States).

National Reverse Mortgage Lenders Association
1625 Massachusetts Ave., NW
Suite 601
Washington, DC 20036
Phone: 1-202-939-1760
Website: http://www.reversemortgage.org/

Cash Surrender Loans

Those with life insurance policies have a number of options available to them when it comes to tapping these policies for money. The first is called a cash-surrender loan, and it's available to those who have permanent life insurance policies that have built up a cash value. With cash surrender loans, you're essentially borrowing against the balance of that cash value (up to 96 percent); the longer the policy has been in place, the more cash value it has and the more you can borrow.

 There are a couple of downsides to reverse mortgages, the most obvious being that the lender, and not your children, will get the house. The lender will also keep track of what you are doing the house with making sure that you continue to live there and pay the taxes and insurance.

Upon your death, the insurance agency gets back whatever you borrowed from your life insurance settlement, plus interest, and then the rest goes to your beneficiaries. Contact your life insurance agent for more information.

Life Settlements

Life settlements are the perfect alternative for those who either can't afford to keep up their premiums or don't wish to do so for some reason. You essentially "sell" your policy to someone else for more cash than the policy is worth. After you die, the person who bought the settlement then gets his or her money back (plus a little more, as the purchaser will buy your settlement for less than it is worth).

For those selling settlements, there is very little risk, as those selling get a check up-front, but you do have to beware of scams or those looking to buy settlements for a fee. There are a few potential downsides, though. You'll need to give the buyer access to your medical records, through which he or she will determine (with the aid of actuary tables) how long you might be expected to live. You'll also have to give permission to the buyer to check with your doctor periodically to see if you're still alive, which might seem a little ghoulish to some. Also, you should consult with your financial planner to see if there are any tax implications, or how such a payment will affect your social security or Medicaid.

Viatical Settlements

Viatical settlements are very similar to life settlements, with this big difference: The person selling the policy is terminally ill and only expected to live two years or less. These are often used to cover medical bills for something like cancer, and you tend to get more than you would from life settlements simply because the buyer is assured of getting his or her money back fairly quickly.

Health

Long-Term Care Insurance

Declining health is something many of us will have to face as we get older, and it can quickly eat up everything you've worked for your whole life if you aren't prepared for it. Long-term care insurance is particularly good to have if you have a lot of assets you wish to protect. Policies of this nature can vary wildly in what they cover (nursing homes? home health care? assisted living?), the premiums you pay, and even whether the policy has some form of inflation protection built in to cover the sharply rising price of health care. You can get this insurance on your own, but check as well to see if your employer (if applicable) has it, as a group plan will probably save on the cost considerably.

You can get more information on this insurance plan through America's Health Insurance Plans' free booklet "Guide to Long-Term Insurance." Contact this organization via the information below, or you can download the booklet from its website.

America's Health Insurance Plans
601 Pennsylvania Avenue, NW
South Building
Suite 500
Washington, DC 20004
Phone: 1-202-778-3200
Fax: 1-202-331-7487
Website: http://www.ahip.org/
E-mail: ahip@ahip.org

Medicare-Approved Drug Discount Cards

At this writing, the Medicare-Approved Drug Discount Card Program is in its infancy, and given that it is slated to be phased out on January 1, 2006 (when the Medicare Drug Benefit plan kicks in), this is a tip with a short shelf life. It's also a confusing one, but for those it applies to, there are benefits.

First, you must have Medicare part A or part B, and not have any other outpatient drug coverage. You can only hold one card at a time, and there are many to choose from . . . twenty eight to be exact, each one offering discounts on a variety of medications at a variety of prices. Enrollment fees on these cards can run up to $30, although lower-income participants can get this fee waved (and also be eligible for a credit on medications worth several hundred dollars).

Because these cards vary so widely in the medications they cover, and even how much you'll pay for said medications under each, it's a good idea to shop around. Talk to your pharmacist, or better yet, get in touch with Medicare and check out its free "Guide to Choosing a Medicare-Approved Drug Discount Card" pamphlet. The Medicare website also offers a very comprehensive comparison chart, where you can enter the medications you take and see which cards cover them and how much they'll cost.

Medicare
Phone: 1-800-MEDICARE
Website: http://www.medicare.gov

Eldercare Locator

The Eldercare Locator is a service of the U.S. Administration on Aging that "connects older Americans and their caregivers with sources of information on senior services." Some of the state and local services it connects you with include: housing, home health services, home delivered meals, legal assistance, and adult day programs/ respite services. This is a fantastic public service that can point you to a wealth of resources to save you money when it comes to eldercare.

Administration on Aging
Washington, DC 20201
Phone: 1-800-677-1116 M-F 9-8, EST (or leave a message)
Website: http://www.eldercare.gov

BenefitsCheckUp.com

These few remaining tips are for those who have access to the Internet. The first is BenefitsCheckUp, a service of the National Council on the Aging. The site is essentially a database of over 1,200 programs across the country that help those over fifty five save on prescription drugs, health care, utilities, and other essential items or services. To use the site, you fill out a free, confidential questionnaire and push a button to submit it to BenefitsCheckUp. The site will then return on-average fifty - seventy money-saving programs in your area.

BenefitsCheckUp
Website: http://www.benefitscheckup.org/

MedicareNewsWatch.com

Another senior health site stocked with resources is MedicareNewsWatch.com (formerly HMOs4Seniors.com). Enter your zip code on the site and you'll not only be able to compare costs for independent Medicare HMO/PPOs in your area, but you can also request information concerning these directly from the website. The site has information on over 100 Medicare HMO/PPOs and offers a number of other perks, including cost comparison reports for major cities and a section providing tips on selecting an HMO.

MedicareNewsWatch.com
Website: http://www. MedicareNewsWatch.com

Additional Web Sites

FirstGov for Seniors

A website that pulls together pretty much every resource that the government maintains for seniors is FirstGov for Seniors. The sections you'll find here include: consumer protection, listings of federal and state agencies, information on retirement, taxes and money, and much more.

> FirstGov for Seniors
> Phone: 1-800-FED-INFO (1-800-333-4636)
> Website: http://www.firstgov.gov/Topics/Seniors.shtml

ThirdAge.com

Another massive "portal" of information for seniors is ThirdAge.com. In addition to an article-packed money section, it also covers topics such as health, travel, beauty, and style.

> ThirdAge Inc.
> 210 Lincoln Street
> Suite 302
> Boston, MA 02111
> Website: http://www.thirdage.com/

18
Other Resources

The following resources offer a broad range of free help and information on everything from consumer issues and product safety to money management and dispute resolution. These resources have been broken down into three sections:

- Government resources: Put the U.S. federal government to work for you! Your tax dollars are responsible for a number of different agencies and other resources that can help you to save money.

- Non-government resources: The federal government isn't the only game in town when it comes to consumer and money information. This section highlights organizations, associations, and other private (and frequently nonprofit) groups that exist to help you in any number of ways.

- Frugal websites: If you have Internet access, you have access to a wealth of frugal articles, tips, free newsletters, and other money-saving information. The websites listed in this section are some of the best available on the Internet.

Government Resources

Consumer Information Catalog

The commercials for the Consumer Information catalog used to be so pervasive that many in the United States would instantly answer "free catalog" when asked what first popped into their minds on hearing the words "Pueblo, Colorado." The Consumer Information catalog is published four times a year by the Government Printing Office and contains in the neighborhood of 200 free or low-cost federal publications that cover topics like employment, small business, education, nutrition, consumer protection, and more. You can order this free catalog by calling, writing them, or visiting the following website.

Consumer Information Catalog
Pueblo, Colorado 81009
Phone: 1-888-8PUEBLO
Website: http://www.pueblo.gsa.gov

Consumer Action Handbook

Think of the Consumer Action Handbook as the Consumer Information catalog on steroids. In publication since 1979, the Consumer Action Handbook contains over 160 pages of information to help you purchase goods and services and avoid some of the pitfalls associated with everything from buying cars to contracting for home improvements. You'll also find a wealth of information on how to successfully solve consumer problems when they arise. This handbook covers everything from contact information for consumer organizations and trade associations to where to turn for help from government agencies on the local, state, and federal level. The handbook also includes a handy sample complaint form that you can use as a template when filling out your own consumer complaint.

The Consumer Action Handbook is available online in its entirety. You can also order a physical copy from the website at http://www.consumeraction.gov, or you can write them at:

> U.S. General Services Administration
> GSA Office of Communications
> Federal Citizen Information Center
> 1800 F Street, NW
> Washington, D.C. 20405

U.S. Consumer Product Safety Commission

Presiding over more than 15,000 types of consumer products, the U.S. Consumer Product Safety Commission's main job is keeping these products from injuring or killing consumers. Over the past thirty years, its work has helped to cut injuries and deaths associated with consumer products by 30 percent. Check with this government office to get the latest information on recalls and other product safety news, or to file your own unsafe product report.

> U.S. Consumer Product Safety Commission
> Washington, D.C. 20207-0001
> Phone: (301)504-7923
> Website: http://www.cpsc.gov
> E-mail: info@cpsc.gov

 The Consumer Information Catalog is published four times a year by the Government Printing Office and contains in the neighborhood of 200 free or low-cost federal publications that cover topics like employment, small business, education, nutrition, consumer protection, and more.

U.S. Department of Housing and Urban Development (HUD)

If it has to do with housing, you'll find information about it at HUD. HUD's mission is to "... increase home ownership, support community development and increase access to affordable housing free, from discrimination." HUD not only oversee's the sale of reduced-price homes, but also maintain's a sizable collection of information on buying, renting, and selling homes. You'll also find much information on home improvements. You can contact HUD at the address below (the web page listed is actually the senior citizen section of their site):

U.S. Department of Housing and Urban Development
451 7th Street S.W.
Washington, DC 20410
Phone: (202)708-1112
TTY: (202)708-1455
Website: http://www.hud.gov/groups/seniors.cfm

Energy Star

Energy Star is a government program that can help individuals and companies save money and help the environment by maximizing efficiency. You can take advantage of its expertise in a couple of different ways. First, when shopping for things such as appliances and other household products (even houses!), look for the Energy Star seal on them. This verifies that the item in question has met strict energy efficiency guidelines set up by the EPA and the U.S. Department of Energy. Second, pay a visit to their website (http://www.energystar.gov) for information on everything from reducing energy costs to the efficient remodeling of kitchens, attics, and more.

FirstGov for Consumers/FirstGov for Seniors

FirstGov is essentially a massive portal that can help you gain access to information buried deep within a wide range of government websites. These cover a number of categories, although the consumers and seniors sections are most relevant for our purposes here. FirstGov for Consumers links to a variety of articles on topics such as food, health, product safety, money, and transportation. While FirstGov for Seniors covers consumer issues as well, it also dives more deeply into issues of special interest to seniors under categories like retirement and money, laws and regulations, and travel and leisure.

> Federal Citizen Information Center
> Office of Citizen Services and Communications, U.S.
>   General Services Administration
> 1800 F Street, NW
> Washington, D.C. 20405
> Phone: (800)333-4636
> FirstGov for Consumers website: http://www.consumer.gov/
> FirstGov for Seniors website: http://www.seniors.gov/

State, County, and City Government Protection Offices

Local government offices exist to help you mediate complaints, educate you on important legal and other consumer issues, and just generally "cover your back" when you're dealing with businesses. Due to any number of factors (including a thorough knowledge of local laws), these closer-to-home agencies are often a better option for consumers seeking agencies help. You can find contact information for these in your local yellow pages.

Non-Government Resources

Consumers Union

This nonprofit consumer organization is best known for its flagship publication, *Consumer Reports*. Consumers Union researches and tests a wide variety of consumer products and services, including everything from cars to clothing. Because of its independence, it has become one of the most trusted sources for consumer information available.

Consumers Union provides a variety of free information on its website, as well as information on how you can subscribe to *Consumer Reports* to benefit from its full range of work.

> Consumers Union/Consumer Reports
> 101 Truman Avenue
> Yonkers, NY 10703-1057
> Website: http://www.consumerreports.org

Consumer Credit Counseling Services

A division of Money Management International, Consumer Credit Counseling Services ". . . provide budget counseling, educational programs, debt management assistance, and housing counseling." You can access this free service through its website, by phone or by visiting them in person.

> CCCS of the Gulf Coast Area, Inc.
> 9009 West Loop South, Suite 700
> Houston TX 77096
> Phone: (713)923-2227
> Website: http://www.cccsintl.org/

Consumers' Checkbook

Founded in 1974, the nonprofit organization Consumers' Checkbook/The Center for the Study of Services publishes a number of magazines and guides stocked with information for consumers. Its primary publication is *Consumers' CHECKBOOK*, which evaluates the quality and pricing of numerous services (i.e., banks, hospitals, plumbers) in seven different U.S. locales: Boston, Chicago, the Delaware Valley, Puget Sound, San Francisco/Oakland/San Jose, the Twin Cities, and Washington, D.C. It also publishes a number of other guides, including *BARGAINS*, which compares pricing for more than 6,000 models of big-ticket items such as TVs and washing machines. Check out its website (http://www.checkbook.org) for information on all the publications and services it offers.

The Better Business Bureau

Established in 1912, the Better Business Bureau (BBB) offers consumers a number of different services to help them in their dealings with businesses. It is probably best known for its dispute resolution efforts. Consumers who have a problem with a company can file a complaint with the BBB, and it will contact the company and attempt to resolve it. Because the organization receives and stores so much feedback on companies, it is also the place to turn before you deal with a business, organization, or other entity that wants your money.

 Consumers who have a problem with a company can file a complaint with the BBB, and it will contact the company and attempt to resolve it. Because it receives and stores so much feedback on companies, it is also the place to turn before you deal with a business, organization, or other entity that wants your money.

The BBB isn't actually a single organization, but rather a series of local organizations made up of businesses. Because the BBB is funded by these businesses, is does not actually recommend specific ones, but it provides feedback and help in the resolution of consumer/ business disputes. Other areas in which it actively participates include the enforcement of truthful advertising and the investigation and ex- posure of fraud against both consumers and businesses.

When contacting the BBB, your best bet is probably to contact the one local to you. You should be able to find this information in your phone book, or you can visit the BBB online (see the address below) to find local BBBs across the United States and Canada. The following contact information is for The Council of Better Business Bureaus, the office that oversees the entire network of BBBs:

The Council of Better Business Bureaus
4200 Wilson Blvd., Suite 800
Arlington VA 22203-1838
Phone: 1(703)276-0100
Fax: 1(703)525-8277
Website: http://www.bbb.org/

National Fraud Information Center/ Internet Fraud Watch

Run by the National Consumers League, the National Fraud Information Center/Internet Fraud Watch covers a number of areas in which fraud and other scams can occur. These include telemarketing fraud, Internet-specific fraud, elder fraud, and information on counter- feit drugs. If something sounds too good to be true, stop by its web- site or call them to check it out. You can also log your own complaint with this organization if you think you have been the victim of fraud or a scam.

Phone: (800)876-7060

Website: http://www.fraud.org

Consumer World

Consumer World bills itself as a "... public service, noncommercial guide with over 2,000 of the most useful consumer resources." This one-stop shopping resource features consumer news, shopping bargains, product reviews, and an extensive directory with contact information for many corporations and government agencies dealing with consumer issues. You can find Consumer World at http://www.consumerworld.org/.

Credit Reports

Regardless of whether you're going to apply for a credit card or a mortgage, you can be assured that the institution you're dealing with is going to check your credit record. This portfolio essentially contains information covering all aspects of your life, from where you live and work, to how much you owe (and to whom). Institutions use these reports to determine how much of a risk you are, creditwise, and sometimes errors can sneak onto your report that can make it very hard to get credit of any kind. As such, it's a good idea to keep a periodic eye on your report so that you know exactly what it contains.

As of September 1, 2005, you can do this for free by contacting one of the top three Consumer Report Agencies listed below:

- Equifax: (800)685-1111 (http://www.equifax.com)
- Experian: (888)397-3742 (http://www.experian.com)
- TransUnion: (800)916-8800 (http://www.transunion.com)

Legal Resources

A number of resources exist for those looking for free legal information or help. For general information, hop onto the Internet and check out one of the following sites:

- American Bar Association (http://www.abalawinfo.org)
- USLaw.com (http://www.uslaw.com)
- TheLaw.com (http://www.thelaw.com)
- FreeAdvice (http://www.freeadvice.com)
- Nolo (http://www.nolo.com)

The National Legal Aid and Defender Association and LSC Public Affairs can both help you to find free legal help covering everything from foreclosures to social security issues. Check your local phone book for the office nearest you, or you can contact their national offices at the addresses listed below:

National Legal Aid and Defender Association
1625 K Street, NW, 8th Floor
Washington, DC 20006
Phone: (202)452-0620
Fax: (202)872-1031
E-mail: info@nlada.org
Website: http://www.nlada.org/

LSC Public Affairs
3333 K St., NW, 3rd Floor
Washington, DC 20007
Phone: (202)295-1500
Fax: (202)337-6797
Website: http://www.lsc.gov/

Frugal Web Sites

All Things Frugal

All Things Frugal houses a number of money-saving resources on its site that includes tips, articles, and links to free stuff, but it is best known for a pair of free frugal publications. The weekly *PennyPincher E-Zine* is stocked with money-saving tips, while the more frequent *Tightwad Tidbits Daily* will bring a new frugal tip into your e-mail box every day. You can subscribe to both at http://www.allthingsfrugal.com.

The Frugal Life

The Frugal Life's slogan, "Living Well with What You Have," is supported on this site by a variety of articles and tips in areas such as autos, cooking, finances, and gardening. It also publishes a number of newsletters on topics such as finances, health, and nature. This website is located at http://www.thefrugallife.com.

Frugal U.

Run by Bankrate.com, Frugal U. offers articles on a number of topics, many of them (not surprisingly) dealing with financial matters. Other areas covered at this site include shopping, pets, and travel. You can find it at http://www.bankrate.com/brm/cheap_home.asp.

Frugal Homemaker

What else would you expect from a site called Frugal Homemaker but . . . frugal articles and tips for homemakers. Its slogan is "Creative, practical and fun ideas for your home!", and this covers a number of areas, from budgeting and organizing a home, to decorating and making simple crafts and gifts. Like many of the other sites listed here, it too offers a free newsletter that you can sign up for. The Frugal Homemaker is located at http://www.frugalhomemaker.com.

The Frugal Village

The Frugal Village is a much more community-oriented site than a lot of others listed here, offering forums, a community cookbook, and even free auctions. Its "Back to Basics" approach includes tips and articles in areas such as simple living, frugality, crafts, homesteading, and traditional skills. You can find it at http://www.frugalvillage.com.

FrugalFun.com

FrugalFun.com concentrates on finances and other frugal areas through its online *Frugal and Fashionable Living Magazine*. It also runs a number of other sites that target more hard-core topics such as frugal marketing and business. You can find the *Frugal and Fashionable Living Magazine* (and links to the above-mentioned other sites) at http://www.frugalfun.com.

The Dollar Stretcher

Unequaled on the Internet in terms of size, The Dollar Stretcher

 All Things Frugal houses a number of money-saving resources on its site that includes tips, articles, and links to free stuff, but it is best known for a pair of free frugal publications. The weekly *PennyPincher E-Zine* is stocked with money-saving tips, while the more frequent *Tightwad Tidbits Daily* will bring a new frugal tip into your e-mail box every day. You can subscribe to both at http://www.allthingsfrugal.com.

offers up hundreds of articles covering everything from mortgages and home repair to weddings and natural living. This site is located at http://www.stretcher.com/index.cfm.

About.com's Frugal Living

One of the pioneers in online frugal information, the Frugal Living section of About.com is packed with articles and tips arranged by topics that include Make It and Fit It, Inspiration and Philosophy, Fun and Leisure, Consumerism, and Dealing With Money. The Frugal Living site can be found at http://frugalliving.about.com.

Frugal Corner

Frugal Corner is actually the home of the Internet chat group misc.consumers.frugal-living. You'll find a wealth of links here to areas such at automobiles, bicycles and other transportation, medical, and camping and outdoor living. Stop in to visit this busy group's website at http://www.frugalcorner.com.

About the Author

Rich Gray has written for *Smart Computing Magazine*, *Woman's Day*, *Sky*, and other magazines. *The Frugal Senior* is his third book.